The Universe and I
My role in the unfolding energies of life

Patrick Quanten
with
Rob Ryder

Copyright © Patrick Quanten 2025

All Rights Reserved. This book is sold subject to the condition that it shall not, by way of trade or otherwise, be resold, hired out, or otherwise circulated without the publisher's prior consent in any form of binding or cover other than that in which it is published and without a similar condition including this condition being imposed on the subsequent publisher. The moral right of Patrick Quanten has been asserted.

Front cover design by Alexander Tull

Every person has free choice. Free to obey or disobey the Natural Laws. Your choice determines the consequences. Nobody ever did, or ever will, escape the consequences of his choices.
- Alfred Armand Montapert

Contents

Introduction	5
The Creation	13
The Universe	14
The creation of matter	15
The creation of life	17
A few concepts	19
The Structure of Life	21
Conception	26
The seed	29
The Development of a Human Being	31
The Function of Life	40
Energy interferences	44
Functioning matter	48
Functioning human being	50
Awareness – Consciousness	55
The unconscious mind	56
The conscious mind	59
Our Reality	62
Life how it has been structured	64
Dreaming	69
Behaviour	74
The mind	75
Behaviour	77
Behavioural disorders	79
Accidents	84
Trauma	91
Childhood trauma	95
Stages of Life	100
Moving Forward	107
Links	115

Introduction

Since 2014 I have been working regularly with Patrick. I contacted him via Magda Taylor who runs 'The Informed Parent' where Patrick writes regular articles. I had been asked by UKColumn News if they could interview me regarding my research into the alleged safety and effectiveness of vaccination, research I had been doing since 2011. My research was very basic and focused on data and even though I had a good understanding of the basic science of 'infections', I felt the interview should be done with someone who had a medical scientific background. Patrick's articles put the scientific clarity into my research, so the better idea was that I interviewed Patrick. It was all arranged and the interview turned out to be a success, even if it was a little before its time, as most of the population were not ready to delve into this fringe idea we now call 'terrain theory'. The theory had been around a long time, in fact even before Pasteur declared 'germ theory' scientific fact, but since 'the pandemic' this notion of the importance of the terrain in infections has had a huge upsurge in interest, to the point it is not far off breaking into mainstream conversation.

Patrick continued to come over yearly to speak at events I arranged locally and to further our understanding of the human condition. Whilst most people, even in natural therapies, were still talking about the physical 'things' of life, Patrick consistently spoke about energetic exchanges and influences. This stirred up my interest massively as I knew all the information that was focusing on the physical stuff was getting very limited results. There simply was no consistency in the thinking and the outcomes. Patrick had always managed to find an energetic reason for a physical manifestation and so my train of thought was pushed more and more into energetic thinking.

I was no stranger to understanding energetic communication. Since 2007 I had been almost obsessed with the television programme *Cesar Millan, The Dog Whisperer*. I had my own love and connection to dogs and I completely understood what he was talking about when he stated it was all about *calm assertive energy*. This is how dogs in a pack communicate. There is a strict hierarchy, led by the pack leader, but it is one of competence and not of power, although he would have that physical power if needed. He dominated though by his mere presence and everyone in the pack respected him, not feared him, but accepted him as the one would lead and protect them. He, the pack leader, was what we used to have in human society, a public servant, or in this case a servant of the pack. His communication to the pack was nearly always energetic and they understood his ear movement, his stance, his tail position and even more his stare. Even when he had to discipline a member of the pack he used the minimum amount of physical force. Simply pinning a disruptive pack member on the ground and staring seriously into the eyes was nearly always enough to get the message across, and he would not move until that message did get across.

I personally used these methods with many dogs I came cross whilst working and I can tell you 100% this energetic conversation works. It even saved me from a mauling when, at a country house where I was doing an outside clean, the owners' two dogs escaped, one a Labrador and one a large rescue German Sheppard. The German Sheppard came out of the house - the owners were out - and ran at me with fangs ready to bite. I turned around and stamped on the ground and pushed him back with my work soap applicator. The Labrador saw this engagement and ran back in. He clearly wasn't after any trouble. I then continued to have an energy fight with this aggressive animal for over 20 minutes. Not once did he touch me. I fended him off with at first an aggressive reaction, but after that I just held my ground, remembering all Cesar Millan had stated, and made myself big, chest out, eyes fixed on him. All in a calm and assertive manner, never aggressive. When he lunged I moved and responded with my own energetic push. After about 20 minutes, he started to get tired and I knew it was over. They can only stay in that aggressive state for so long as it uses up too much energy. He eventually backed off, laid down, keeping me in his sight from about 15 meters away, panting and then the moment I had been waiting for, his ears dropped. He was done, and without a single physical strike on either side I was victorious. I turned my back on him and continued to go up my ladder and spend about half an hour cleaning the windows of this country house without him even offering me a growl. This is why I knew Patrick was onto something when he was always explaining things in terms of energetic exchanges.

In fact, I can say there are two categories of dog that will attack me whilst I am working. One is a dog that, because of a lack of leadership from the human 'boss', has taken it upon itself to be the pack leader, the protector. This is like putting a child in charge of house security. They simply do not have the knowledge and experience to fulfil that role and such a situation can only end in disaster. The other type, and more significant to what Patrick will write about, is a dog that has been rescued from a violent home. The dog is traumatised and has learnt to be in fear of its environment, especially in contact with humans. This type of dog gets rescued but the new owner feels sorry for it and energetically that means that its environment has not changed very much. The dog in reality is searching for safety and leadership to move on from the past but the constant feeling sorry for him means he is kept in that fearful state. The dog will continue to be aggressive when encountering people or certain situations and instead of saying assertively 'hey, we don't need to do that here, I'm in charge now', communicated via actions and energy, people comfort the dog in that fearful aggressive state. To the dog that means that it is still okay to be afraid and aggressive. This simply means the dog continues to live in a traumatic state as for him the environment has not changed and what he really needs is the human, the pack leader, to take control and show him life has moved on and the state of danger is over. As Cesar Millan says, only pet a dog when it is doing the behaviour you want and ignore or address the behaviour you do not want.

My own search for truth and understanding life and society got a huge boost at the 2008 financial crash. I had observed the power of big banks and corporations in my time in Latin America and the huge, and seemingly unjust, divide between very rich and the poverty of the masses, which was very clear to see when I was travelling around and living in South America. But when I felt I was not being told the truth about the financial crash, I decided to research more and the veil of smog surrounding economics was lifted when I came to understand how money/currency was created, as a deliberate unpayable debt, to enslave people and nations and to suck the assets and wealth into the hands of an unaccountable few. Within a very short period of time the whole global control agenda was laid out on front of me.

This agenda is described in our book *'A Conscious Humanity – Morality, Freedom and Natural Law'*. It focuses on a simple understanding of the present human condition and exposes the illusionary nature of the political system that controls us all. Together with other books we have both published, it paints a very detailed picture of the situation humanity is in now. Without a deep understanding of the problem we can never find a solution.

In 2024, I asked Patrick to come over for one last time to bring everything together in a seminar to try and show people what he had been talking about for years, everything is an exchange of energy. The government imposed terror of 'The Lockdown' had acted like a homeopathic message to those who were ready to receive it. Humanity was enslaved by an elite class of people who believe they are our masters. The message of the lockdown had woken many people to this truth but not enough to change the status quo. The critical mass, needed to change society, had not been reached as yet; though once you can see this information, it is hard to un-see it, so the numbers can only rise. The number of people, traumatised by the madness of that era and that had contracted even more into solidly believing in 'The System', had also increased. And it is these people, it seemed, that have had the loudest voices and the strongest influence, all manipulated of course. The stalemate will continue to go on for a while and even though I continue to speak to people and put out information the main focus now is on my own personal life, my family and community.

As explained in the '*Conscious Humanity*' book, the endgame of the controlling elite is total control of humanity via technology and illusionary rules. 'They', however, are not brave enough to just come out and say this, so they sell it as bringing power to local communities, devolution and less central government power, which they call 'Communitarianism'. What it actually is, is central control wrapped up as community power. If you want to sell a rotten maggot pie then you have to cover it in strawberries and cream. This means their plan cannot work if local communities do not go along with it and this means that the only politics we have to get involved with are the politics of our own local community. So now I do not have to concern myself with the goings on of other people's problems on the other side of the world. In fact, I do not even need to bother about the issues facing other people on the other side of my country. As it should be, my only concern is now my own family and community. So I will continue to put out information locally but I also need to focus on my own life first.

The global agenda is to create communities of weak people that can be easily controlled. They do not want communities of strong individuals who want to improve their lives and create strong communities capable of independent thinking and action. The solution to dependency is to be independent and the solution to being reliant on others is to be self-reliant. Communities made of strong individuals are very difficult to control and what is known as the 'Woke Agenda' is a specific attack on the minds of humanity to elevate weak and narcissistic people into positions of power and leadership in central and local government.

In a pride of lions, or a pack of wolves, this would not be tolerated as it would put the existence of the whole group at risk. The hierarchy exists not for elevating power alone but for elevating competency. It is this competency that provides a future for the group and in a group like this the weaker ones will find their place and be provided for. In times past, it was the wise elders in the community or the Shaman of tribal people whose job it was to keep the structure of the community balanced and to keep power in the hands of the strong and competent. Sadly, this traditional type of organised community leadership has been destroyed and *chosen* leaders have been trained and put in their place. Popularity vote chosen over competence. So the only politics we need to get involved in is local politics, but with an awareness of a global agenda sneaking in to control.

To really make positive impact in our community we first need to become empowered ourselves as individuals and to do this we need to delve deeper into the human condition and see our behaviour for what it is, an energetic field expressing itself into 'physical' behaviour. We also need to look more into our own minds as that is where we will gain insight into this behaviour and the thoughts, feelings and emotions behind it. There are far too many people going around telling others what they need to do whilst not having their own house in order. To lead a community, we need to lead by example and not by the words coming out of our mouths, as actions tell far more about a person than his words. It is our deeds that have a longer impact in our life and the lives of others. 'Talking the talk' is fine but not worth much if we do not 'walk the walk'. In fact when we act in truth and in balance, it speaks our words for us. Actions do speak louder than words after all.

The seminar was done and recorded and put up on YouTube and we managed 13 extra conversations out of that seminar which we also published on YouTube. The theme all along was to understand the forces that create everything in the universe, including ourselves, and to delve into the bigger mystery of the human mind. The challenge now was to put this altogether in a book and focus totally on the energy. Science has told us $E=mc^2$, meaning matter is equal to the energy. As we know the universe is made up from energy, including the matter itself, it seems logical to focus on what that energy is. For the matter to change, the energy field has to change first. Yet most of the activity in the world is focused on the physical matter. Even neuroscientists are trying to explain the brain through physical activity and many claim eventually they will explain consciousness itself as a physical thing in the brain.

The double slit experiment and its meaning is also something not even close to being agreed upon in science. Most say *consciousness* or *observing* or *measuring* the waveform causes it to collapse from an energetic possibility to an actual 'thing', a particle. The problem with this is that if the particle were real, then space would be real and we would have the problem of explaining infinity. A few think there is no collapse at all but this would not explain the classical, physical, world around us.

But what if neither were wrong or right but that the collapse was a *perceived* collapse? This would end the need to explain infinity because reality would not come into *actual* existence via observation but would be *perceived* into existence. This not only does away with the need to explain infinite space but shows us again that reality is at all times energetic. So again, if we want to impact the 'physical', we need to focus on the 'energetic'. This experiment has also been hijacked by the New Age to promote the idea of us 'creating our own reality'. I say hijacked, because it turns people away from confronting their *actual* reality and life and believing all they have to do is to change their focus and they can manifest anything they want. It is a form of avoidance and though I believe there is possibility in our own minds to affect our own reality and experiences, I feel Patrick's explanation of this will be far more practical and more grounded in truth and not at all grounded in avoiding what life is really trying to tell us. Every 'thing' in life is a receiver and transmitter of information/energy. This constant exchange creates what we call *cause and effect*. Every cause creates an effect and that effect becomes the next cause for the next effect and so on, so let's try and find out what that actually means.

> *We were ALL morons once. We were what we were before and we are what we are now. If we weren't what we were before we would not be what we are now and we are probably what we are now, BECAUSE of what we were before, and without what we were before and what we are now, we can never be what we will be.*

Beyond ego

When most people talk about evolution, they, more often than not, mention the physical things in the universe constantly changing or more so life on earth changing constantly in all its diversity. Again, it is all about physical life. But as we will see, life is but an expression of energy, and it seems that from the moment of creation, 'things' have been evolving to the point where we are now able to question this process as human life on this planet. We, as human beings and part of nature, are able to ponder on our existence and everything around us and try to find meaning. Just as a baby, when conceived, is put on a path to grow and develop, so is everything else. If you feel the need to go on your own journey of self-discovery then I suggest you better start on a blank page.

All institutions have now been infiltrated and, so it seems, have inverted real truth. If some self-proclaimed authority now tells me something, a fact, it has got to the point where it seems the total opposite will be closer to the truth and a better starting point for my investigation.

> *"They must find it difficult, those who have taken authority as truth, rather than truth as authority."*   - Gerald Massey

This quote shows us exactly where we are as a society. Authority in society is a position of power and control, and truth just gets in the way. In nature, truth is the authority and there is no contradiction. So in an upside down and totally corrupted world, the only place to go and seek real truth is the nature that created us and that we are part of. This is why many spiritual practices teach people to go within.

Where does an individual need to start to understand his/her own individual evolution and what it is to be part of a whole?

My own personal starting point was a very blunt shock to the system, brought about by a moment of being conscious about my own behaviour and its consequences for myself and others. The reality that I was a 'moron' entered my consciousness.

During our time living in the Peruvian Amazon in Iquitos, mosquitoes seemed to thrive on making sleep impossible with their constant harassment. At night, we sprayed our rooms with a spray we were told was toxic to this mortal enemy of sleep. We sprayed the doors, the mosquito net and the window frames. The name of the spray did not seem relevant at the time; our only focus was a good night's sleep. A few years later and living back in England, I had my 'light bulb moment' amidst the 2008 financial crash. The name of the spray was *'mata todo'*, which in English translates as *'kills everything'*. Yes, everything! Meaning all biological life of which we are all a part, including me. What an absolute moron!!

When the informational attack flooded my mind after 2008, I downloaded masses of information in a short time which contradicted almost everything I once thought was true. Indeed life, the world, and myself in it, was now to be seen in a totally new way. I did not realise it at the time but not once did I feel stupid for being previously wrong or not once did my ego fight to hold on to its integrity. My thirst for truth completely overpowered any resistance of my ego and of engrained beliefs. I naively thought all I had to do is give people this clear irrefutable information and they too would see it, embrace it, and in no time at all there would be a world-wide revolution of truth and peace. 'Easy peasy lemon squeezy', as they say! Obviously that is not what happened. It took me a long time to understand the power of ingrained beliefs and the resistance of the ego to admit it is not even nearly as clever as it thinks it is.

This made me see the real attack on humanity is the attack on consciousness and that the real evolution is *'The Evolution of Consciousness via Experience'*. So, if humanity is an evolving species, and evolution is about evolving our consciousness and our minds via experience, and we are nowhere near enlightened, then we have to accept we all have a long way to go. We are not even at the stage where we can say we can confidently inflict society with our perceived intelligence, as the results do not lie. Technology, and the intelligence behind it, has not made the world a better place, a bit more comfortable maybe, but certainly not more peaceful. We are at a stage of trying to become more aware, more conscious and sadly we need more experience, a lot more experience. So we could state that at the present time *the evolution of being less stupid* is a more appropriate acknowledgment of where we all are.

So we come back now to the project and challenge I have given Patrick, which is to explain life totally via energy and natural forces in and around us and to explain the nature of the human mind.

- What are the forces that create life?
- What is it to be aware?
- What is it to be conscious?
- How do we connect the conscious and unconscious mind?

If we want to act in a way that is in balance with ourselves and compatible with freedom in our local community, we need the tools and the understanding to go inside ourselves. We need to see what energy there is, how it works and how we can use this to manifest behaviour that promotes wellbeing for ourselves and for those around us, as this behaviour is the end product of an energetic process that starts within.

How do our personal effects/responses to life around us create causes that feed other effects around us?

Can all this information be put together in one idea and have practical use for our lives?

I will now hand you over to Patrick to give a detailed look at the forces that control our life, all of life, and to put some clarity on what is driving our lives to become more conscious through experience. Stay with the process, as we hope to bring it all together at the end to put forward simple, practical ways to improve our own life path and to keep the balance a more comfortable one. It won't be an end to challenges but we may see those challenges in a new light and be able to consciously make better decisions that are more in balance with where our life wants to go and not where we, the ego, thinks it should be going.

Chapter 1

The Creation

When you understand how something has been made, you know how it functions and you can fairly easily identify why it goes wrong. This is true for mechanical things humans produce as well as for life itself. Understanding life means that you know how it has been created. 'Fixing' life, restoring health and balance in life, can only truly be done when you understand life, when you understand what it is and how it operates. And this is the simple explanation why our allopathic medical system is a complete failure with regards to managing the health of the individual and the population. Over the last few decades, this has become even more obvious as the medical authorities, together with all other authorities, have chosen the path of artificial over life itself. Not only is life being judged and managed via computer models rather than via observation of real life, but we are even praising intelligence as something artificial. Artificial intelligence has more value in life, has more to offer to human life, than human or intuitive intelligence. Pretending to understand life and using this pretence to fiddle with the building blocks of life is a recipe for disaster.

You don't have to believe me, but let me take you on a journey that has its roots firmly fixed in scientific truth and that will reveal a lot more about life and the way it functions. In order to understand how it is made we need to have an idea about what creation truly is and how it comes about.

Creation means 'the act of making or producing something that did not exist before'. While much of popular culture paints creativity as a privilege of artists and inventors, everyday creativity is different. It's the parent figuring out how to feed three kids with half a pantry. The elder who repurposes old sweaters into quilts. The neighbour who turns a tiny yard into a community garden using buckets and broken planters. Studies in positive psychology, such as those by Dr. Ruth Richards at Harvard, highlight that 'everyday creativity' plays a crucial role in resilience and mental well-being. It's not just an outlet; it's a lifeline. Necessity isn't just the mother of invention; it's the midwife of meaning. Creation is driven by purpose, by meaning. It isn't a random thing happening out of the blue. It is a meaningful act, and it is this meaning we need to comprehend if we ever want to understand life.

Creating something out of nothing, 'out of thin air', is a concept used to denote God's work in creation. In fact, science tells us that you cannot create something out of nothing, but not understanding how the creation, the universe, came into being begs for a 'deus ex machina', a magical hand that manifests something out of nothing. The truth is that once we have that initial universe – where in God's name did it come from? – everything that comes into existence from that point onwards, we do believe needs to be explained in the form of a process rooted in what was already there. Then the question arises, why would the universe itself be any different?

It is more logical to assume that the universe itself was also created out of something, just as all the rest of creation, than it is to assume that the universe itself is something special, operating by adhering to different rules and creative laws than everything in it. What exactly it is that was already there and from which the universe was created, is not really necessary to know in order to make sense of what the universe has created. In fact, by understanding the creation within the universe and our assumption that everything is the same and follows the same action patterns, it will become much easier to deduct what the substrate is from which the universe came forth.

The universe

The universe is essentially an energy field. It is a bubble that floats around, which indicates that it is surrounded by, and is part of, another energy field. Think about it in terms of a soap bubble floating around in the air. The inside of the soap bubble is our universe and the air is the energy field that is holding the universe and from which it stems. Take note of the fact that the soap bubble moves around, both in the air, where it takes up different positions all the time, and moves inside, whereby the shape of the soap bubble changes constantly. This is due to a constant change of pressure inside the bubble, which pushes the air inside the bubble around, in balance with the varying pressure from the air around the bubble. These changing pressures are responsible for the movement of the energy inside the bubble as well as for the movement of the entire bubble in the surrounding air

We know that the universe is filled with energy and that the energy inside the universe moves constantly. This can only occur when the energy that is locked inside the universe is in places contracting and in other places expanding. Science has shown that there are three basic forces at work within the universe, three basic 'types' of energy motion. First of all, there is the constantly present energy, which is referred to as 'life energy'. This is the energy that is responsible for 'filling' the universe bubble, for making it happen in the first place. Besides this energy, and constantly interacting with this energy, are two other forces. One is called the strong force, which is pushing parts of the energy field together, making it contract, and the other is the weak force, which is pushing parts of the energy field apart, making it expand. Hence, the universe contains three forces: the life force, the contracting force and the expansive force. Everything that happens within the energy field of the universe is a result of the interaction between these three forces.

Changing pressures in localised areas within the universe upon that area will prompt the energy to either contract, due to increased pressure, or expand, due to decreased pressure. However, just as is the case with our soap bubble, the temperature in localised parts within the field also plays a part in the movement of the energy. Lower temperature will make the energy contract, while higher temperature will make it expand. That is why the air within an air balloon is being warmed, which will make the air less dense, more expansive. This allows the balloon to move through the outside air in an upwards direction. When a specific part of the universe contracts, it will expand somewhere else as the total amount of energy present within the universe remains the same. No energy is lost and no energy is created within the universe. All that happens to the universal energy is that it changes, due to the impact of the contracting and expanding forces.

There is a constant balance in the movement of energies within the universe. When this balance gets broken, the bubble bursts, the universe explodes. As we are still here and still experiencing the universe holding us together, we must assume that the universal energies are in balance, that all the movement of all elements within the universe is balanced, is compensated for by movement in the opposite direction elsewhere. If it contracts in one area, it expands in another. If it cools down in one area, it warms up in another.

The creation of matter

Within this universal energy field we notice that matter is present in very specific, but small, areas. In physics, matter is the substance that makes up the observable universe. Along with energy, it forms the basis of all objective phenomena. At its most fundamental level, matter consists of elementary particles called quarks and leptons, which include electrons. Quarks combine to form protons and neutrons. Protons, neutrons, and electrons form atoms, which are the building blocks of elements like hydrogen, oxygen, and iron. Atoms can combine to form molecules, and large groups of atoms or molecules form the bulk matter of everyday life. All matter shares the fundamental property of inertia, which resists changes in its state of motion. In other words, tiny particles are being formed, which combine to become larger particles, which lock together to become even larger particles of matter. Matter sticks together and becomes inert. It loses the ability of much internal movement. The particles themselves still move around but a small part of the energetic field that forms the inner world of the particle has become stationary, resistant to change. As a result of contraction, the space in which that part of the energy field moves becomes smaller and smaller until it appears to fill one point in space. That small part of the energy field takes on a certain form and it remains that way, which is different from the constant motion of the rest of energy field. As such, it becomes 'separated' from the rest of the energy field, while in essence it still remains an integral part of that field. That specific point in the energy field manifests. It becomes matter. It becomes the 'observable universe'. It is like the frozen crystal that appears out of the water mass, fixing a small part of fluid water into a solid element.

Becoming less mobile is a result of contracting energies. Energies become 'heavier', more dense, due to an increase in pressure on that part of the field or due to a decrease in temperature, which will 'freeze' the energy. When that part, a tiny part, of the energy field becomes, what we observe as, immobile, the vibrating energy gets 'fixed' into a point. The energy wave is being compressed to the extent that it vibrates up and down on the spot, the point of matter creation. This is the point where the tiniest particles of matter are being manifested. A tiny part of the energy field has contracted into a point and the energy held within that point is no longer able to escape that point or 'to mix' directly and freely with other energies of the field. That point remains the same, at least for some time, for as long as the inside energy structure is balanced with the ever changing energies that surround it. That point is the materialisation of energy.

As the pressure on the immediate surroundings of that point keeps increasing and/or the temperature inside the point keeps dropping, the point continues to contract, whereby more of the energy from the immediate surroundings is being pushed onto the initial point. This will create combined material structures, forming atoms, that will combine into molecules and molecules will form larger material structures and various kinds of matter. All this is the direct result of a constantly present high pressure and/or low temperature. One 'fixed' point in space is being pushed together onto other 'fixed' points to create a ball of fixed points, and then these balls are being pushed together to create matter we can actually observe through our senses. We can observe this process in the way ice is being formed. Water droplets freeze 'onto' a nucleus. This can be a tiny particle of whatever sort within the water, which will form the 'nucleus' around which the water will freeze and become ice. Once there is an ice nucleus, the freezing process develops very quickly. Hence, once a first nucleus of matter has formed within the universe, there will be a rapid 'growth', an expansion, of more matter that attaches itself to this nucleus. Hence the formation sequence of quarks, forming protons and neutrons, forming atoms, forming molecules, forming larger structure of matter.

This matter comes into existence step by step, whereby the density of the matter increases with each step taken, and each step occupies more and more outer space. There are basically three forms of matter that we identify within the universe. The first stage is the creation of gases. Here small particles, mostly single atoms, float around within a bubble that has separated from the rest of the universal energy field. In this separate field these bits of matter still have a lot of room to move but they can no longer make use of the entire universal field. They are 'captured' within a gas cloud. The next stage happens inside this cloud when parts of it become even more dense and take on a liquid form. One could, in this case, speak about 'a cloud of liquid' floating around inside the gas cloud. And the last step in the creation of physical matter is the densification of parts of the liquid cloud into solid matter. Matter manifests in three different forms: gas, liquid, solid. It is important to remember that each subsequent layer of manifestation occurs within the previous, already existing, layer. Gas is a solidification of pure energy. Liquid is a solidification of gas. Solid matter is a solidification of liquid. Put this in terms of the earth then it must be obvious that the solid parts, the rocks and the soil and the sand, are created out of the liquids on earth, amongst others the waters of the earth, and that the oceans were the original densification of a tiny part of a gas cloud within the solar system, which is still identifiable as the earth's atmosphere.

Matter has been created in parts of the universal energy field. But that is not where the creation story ends.

The creation of life

Just imagine that the pressure still increases, that the temperature still keeps dropping. The building blocks of matter have arranged themselves in the least space occupying form of all constructions and yet the pressure continues. The individual pieces of matter have nowhere to go. There is no further space saving construct that will allow the matter to absorb that increasing contraction force. The internal space within the solid matter has all been used. Matter is on the verge of becoming crushed. And then another magical thing happens!

Some of the tissues, some of the forms within the solid part of creation, that have been created join together in such a way that they are able to absorb the pressure put upon the tissues by creating more tissues, whereby the matter is actually expanding outward into the space surrounding the solid matter, instead of being continuously being pushed together. It creates the illusion that the matter is actually 'growing'. The basic construct that allows such a development, we call a cell. Under the continuing pressure, one cell increases the matter content of all its structures. This leads to a point where the structure is bound to burst under the pressure. However, this part of solid matter is able to separate some of its extra structures off to form a second, identical, structure. In this manner, one cell becomes two, two becomes four and so on, and these cells all stick together, held together by the outside pressure exerted upon the material manifestation. Together they form what we call an organism. The birth of life. The dawn of a complete new era in creation. The newly formed and separated cells lie next to one another and are identical to one another. By producing more and more cells, it appears to us as if that organism is growing. It 'moves' into the space it is surrounded by. It pushes itself into that space, whether we are talking about the roots of the plants that push away the soil or the top of the plant that occupies air-space or water-space, depending on the environment the plant is growing into. Energetic pressure exerted upon the solid mass results in the occupation of a larger space within the manifested part of creation, within the solid, liquid and gas part of the manifestation, of creation.

This line of construction is a separate path, a distinctly different way, to form solid matter. Hence, the pressure upon the liquid state of creation results on the one hand in the manifestation of our known solid matter, but it also gives rise to a structure that forms the basis of what we call 'life-matter'. When gas, liquid and solid matter is put under increasing pressure it contracts, it shrinks, it takes up less space. However, when this new form of solid manifestation, a cell, becomes pressurised by its environment it 'grows', it takes up more space, not less. From unicellular organisms, such as bacteria, it evolves into multicellular organisms, giving rise to plants and later to animals and human beings. Here, once again, the next generation within creation, the next manifestation, is a further development, a further refinement, of the type of organism that went before. Put life under increasing pressure and it will evolve, it will grow, it will adapt.

So let's follow the timeline now. The universe comes into existence. Within specific places of this universe a contraction takes place to create gas clouds. Within specific places of the gas clouds a contraction takes place to create liquid clouds. Within specific places of the liquid clouds a contraction takes place to create solid matter. After some time, within this liquid matter a new arrangement, as a result of higher pressure, creates a lifeform, cellular organisms, as a new solid structure of matter. The first development step of this lifeform is taking place within the solid matter it is an integral part of. Bacteria are found within soil, as well as within water. They are formed because of the more free movement that is available to the basic material building blocks within liquid, but once it is formed it separates from that liquid as a solid form of creation. The first development stage of this newly constructed form is plant life, which is completely rooted within the soil, within the solid part of creation. However, a slight change in cellular structure occurs, which gives rise to the formation of a slightly different cell type. These cells will eventually 'grow' into animal life, which typically differs from plant life in the fact that animals have free movement, free from the soil. They still feed from the soil, and its products, but they are no longer fixed into it by a root system. The development of animal life runs over various easily recognisable stages from egg laying animals to mammals to human beings. Each of those stages can only become manifest when the previous layer has completely used up its potential to adjust to the pressures of life, to the pressures of its surroundings, and requires a fundamental adjustment to the structure in order to have a scope for further expansion.

A few concepts

Now we are able to define certain things more clearly. In the first place, the space that fills the bubble – recall the image of the soap bubble – is energy, is a chaos of waves, is a vibrating field of 'nothingness'. The universal space is energy, and it manifests in this particular bubble because of a specific pressure within itself. However, this apparent nothing can become a lot of things. In other words, the nothingness has 'the potential' to manifest in different ways, to create a lot of different things. Depending on where within that field and how within that field contraction occurs, a different manifestation will appear. 'Nothing' holds the potential for a lot of things. Not for everything, as the energy field always is just a spectrum of energies, of vibrations, of waves, which means that it has an upper and a lower limit. But within that spectrum, all potential is present.

This energy is on the move. The motion is caused by different areas contracting and expanding throughout the field. This results in different pressures over different areas, which moves the energy within the field and the field as a whole, as is obvious from watching the soap bubble move through the air. All movement is the result of pressure differences. All changes are the result of pressure differences. If there are no pressure differences between various areas then there is no flow, no motion, and also no change. In this case, everything would remain the same, forever. In which case there is no life. Life is movement. Life energy needs to flow, and it's the interplay between the contracting and expanding force that creates that movement.

A change is something that is different from what it was. This means that at some point it was a certain way and at another point it became something different. This is the emergence of time. If something is different from one moment in time to another moment, then we have our definition of time. Now we know what time truly is. Time is the result of movement. If there is no movement, there is no time. No motion, no time. It is the motion that creates differences, which are, in turn, linked to a timeline in which they occurred. The succession of these events we call time. One thing happened before another, and after yet another thing. The difference in how long it took to get from one event to the next and then to the following can be compared and put into a fixed schedule, which we call time. Observing the change in the shape of the moon allows us to nominate the period it takes to move from one shape into the next as a certain period of time. One cycle we can call one moon-cycle, or one month. We can do the same with the position the sun occupies in the sky throughout the day. We now have a concept to divide one day and night cycle into shorter time segments, called hours. The long sun cycle moving its position across the sky is called one year. Time isn't a so-called fourth dimension. It is simply the direct result of movement.

Furthermore, the sequence of the creative process shows us that everything that happens is the result of an interaction. It is not about what is in the field that determines what exactly will manifest. The manifestation is the result of the interaction between what is in the field and the impact of the force that makes contact with what already exists in the field. What is already present *changes* as a result of the contraction or expansion force that impacts it. Whatever life manifests is a direct result of the interaction between the makeup of the organism and the impact of the surrounding environment. It is not because a hurricane is racing across the land that all trees will be uprooted. The oak may become uprooted while the palm tree bends in the wind and remains firmly rooted in the soil. The force exerted onto the field is the same but the impact on the elements within the field varies according to the qualities of those elements. It is that impact that ultimately is responsible for the changes that happen within the field, for the evolution of the field. Creation is about changing what is there into something different. And what is already present in the field, already manifested within the field, is not in its entirety going to respond in the same way to pressure exerted upon that field. In human terms, it means that not everything that we are surrounded by, come in contact with, will affect every human being in the same way.

Chapter 2

The Structure of Life

Life begins with the formation of the first cell. This cell is a manifestation of a small part of the spectrum that contains all solid matter. Every part of an energy spectrum is made up out of the same basic energies, the same basic vibrations. A way to understand how this works is offered by the structure of music, the notes. There are seven different notes. It turns out that, when we look closely, the universe, earth and life are all structured based on seven layers, seven subdivisions. Seven notes appear in a fixed order in relation to one another and the group together is called an octave. In fact, an octave consists of eight notes, even though the universe only has seven intrinsic 'different' layers, but the eight note in an octave is the same as the first note, only one octave different. Note 1 and 8 are the same notes, but note 8 has 'moved up' one octave, which means that note 8 has twice the frequency of vibration than note 1. Note 8 forms the last note in one octave and at the same time it is the first note in the following octave. It is an overlapping structure. One octave emerges from, is constructed out of, the previous octave. These basic seven notes, organised in octaves, keep repeating themselves all along an entire spectrum of frequencies of energies. This immediately indicates that all manifestations are formed from the same seven notes and are therefore intrinsically connected with one another. It is all 'the same stuff'.

The physical expression of a particular note is different, depending on which octave it belongs to. Just as in a musical piece, the way the note sounds varies according to the octave it is played in.

We are told that the electromagnetic spectrum includes radio waves, microwaves, infrared, visible light, ultraviolet, x-rays and gamma rays, being seven different 'types' of energies spread out over one octave, the entire spectrum. This is not entirely true. The infrared, the visible light and the ultraviolet are all types of light and are therefore part of one complete set within the electromagnetic spectrum. Sunlight produces two types of ultraviolet light and three types of infrared light. Five different, to us not visible, types of light combine with seven different colours, visible light, to give us a total of twelve different types of light, being one octave. An octave contains seven full notes and five in-between steps, which are not full notes. In music, the distance between notes is called an 'interval'. A semitone in music is the smallest gap, the smallest interval, between two notes, an in-between step. It represents the distance of one half-step between one note and the next one. In short, a whole tone is equivalent to two semitones: two steps between one full note and the next one. Seven full tones, seven light colours. Five semi-tones, divided into one group of three and one group of two; five invisible light bands, three infrared ones and two ultraviolet ones. Hence, we must conclude that scientists know five out of the seven bands that make up the entire electromagnetic spectrum as the ultraviolet and infrared light bands are an integral part of the light spectrum. Hence, the energy spectrum of the universe, as we know it by now, is divided into the following energy bands, from low to high frequencies: radio waves, microwaves, light waves, x-rays and gamma rays. My guess is that there is one more band below the radio waves that we are not aware of, and one more above the gamma rays. Too low and too high for us to measure or to recognise it as a distinctly different group.

Life is created on earth. It manifests within the energies of earth, within the vibrational spectrum of earth, and therefore life is sustained by the frequency spectrum of earth. The Schumann resonances, the electromagnetic harmony of the earth, are a set of spectral peaks in the extremely low frequency portion of the earth's electromagnetic field spectrum. Schumann resonances are the principal background in the part of the electromagnetic spectrum from 3 Hz through 60 Hz and appear as distinct peaks at extremely low frequencies around 7.83 Hz (fundamental), 14.3, 20.8, 27.3, and 33.8 Hz. Life on earth develops within this frequency spectrum, which is at the very low end of the electromagnetic spectrum of the universe, below radio frequencies. Maybe these extreme low frequencies are a separate band and don't belong to the radio frequency band of the electromagnetic spectrum. Maybe this represents the true matter manifestation band within the universal spectrum. But let's not get lost in frequencies and let's focus on the structure of life as it emerges from the energy soup as an almost invisible bubble in the soup bowl.

Energy contracts that much that some of it becomes 'fixed' in matter. The balance of energy, the harmonics of that specific matter, also becomes stuck on the energies that have been 'frozen' into the material particles or the parts that make up the specific cell. In other words, it has a limited range in which it can exist. It is worth noting that within a cell we can recognise seven different structures, organelles, which together create the cell function. Hence, the complete structure of the cell is an expression of one octave, a complete set of notes, that are fixed within a certain frequency band, which is what determines the physical properties of the cell and of the organism. Humans will have the same seven systems as animals have, but the physical expression may vary a lot from most animals, and it has the most in common with animals more recent in their appearance on the evolution chart.

Let's recap how matter becomes manifest. A small part of the field contracts to a point where it becomes matter. This means that only a specific set of energies, a small number of octaves, becomes frozen in that process. It certainly contains all seven notes of the universe, but by no means all octaves that are present within the universe. Only a small number of those make up that piece of matter. It is the harmony we hear in one specific song. As the contraction process continues, we have seen that a small section of the gas cloud, which only has a small number of octaves within it (compared to the almost indefinite number of octaves in the entire universe), becomes even more dense and manifests as a liquid cloud, containing even a smaller number of octaves, selected from the ones that are available within the gas cloud. This in turn contracts to manifest as solid matter, the expression of an even smaller number of octaves selected from within the liquid cloud. A specific set of octaves creates the cell, the basic structure of life. A cell is the fixation of a very narrow band of octaves, which will further express the information that the energy frequencies carry. Each of the seven notes will give rise to one specific physical system, both within the cell and the organism that will grow from it.
These are:
- the lymphatic system
- the circulatory system
- the digestive and respiratory system
- the mobility system
- the sensory system
- the nervous system
- the glandular system

Each octave can be 'identified' by its last note (number 8) and the seven notes that precede this one can be seen as the 'unfolding' of that specific octave, the notes that lay hidden underneath and that support the octave. In life terms, that means that an organism, be it a chicken, a shark, a pig or a human, displays each of the seven systems, but in a different way. The particular way of expression is determined by the species, by the specific octave in which the notes appear, and this will be different if the basic cell is formed within the energetic range that will be expressed as a chicken or as a human being. In the same way, each of these seven systems are being made up out of the same seven tissues, but these appear within each of the systems in a slightly different, but still very recognisable, way or format. The seven tissues, relating to the same 'notes' as the seven systems, are as follows:

- water/skin tissue
- blood tissue
- muscle tissue
- fat tissue
- bone tissue
- nerve tissue
- reproductive tissue

The part of the electromagnetic spectrum within the very small range that is able to form cells determines what kind of cell it is. The structure of a basic animal cell is the same for all animals, but depending on which part of that cell spectrum the cell belongs to, it will develop into a different species of animal. Each of these organisms, the species as well as the individual organism, has a limited range, a fixed energetic balance, in which it can exist, in which life can be sustained. Changing circumstances will require a change within the organism in order to maintain its inner balance and to ensure further life, as more extensive changes within the environment and circumstances may even bring about the demise of an entire species. Just as plants are able to adjust to the seasons, display different responses to different circumstances, animals are also capable of doing this. And just as there is a limit to how much heat or how much cold a specific species of plant can survive in, there also is a limit to the kind of environmental circumstances a specific species of animal can survive in.

Every animal species occupies a specific frequency band on the spectrum, and every individual organism within such one species is an expression of a tiny portion of that frequency band. The differences between the various species are already expressed within the animal cell that will develop into a member of that species. We identify those differences in the genetic makeup of the cell. A tiny portion of the genes contain different sequences of genetic codes. Individual differences between various individual organisms of the same species are expressed in an even smaller number of genetic codes. And yet, all the species and every individual member of all those species develop the same seven systems, made up from the same seven tissues. How a note sounds, how it is being expressed, depends on which octave it is in, but it remains the same note!

It all starts from one cell. When this cell multiplies to create an entire organism, every cell of that organism contains the same information and yet groups of cells express this information in very different ways, resulting in very different tissue cells, making up very different systems. What is responsible for the variety in expressions? It is the interaction of each cell within the cluster of cells in the early stages of the development of the specific organism with the information reaching the cluster from the environment. Although every cell is exposed to the same environment, cells receive the information from the environment differently, depending, amongst other things, on their position within the cluster. We can get an idea about how this works by looking at how we draw the plans for building our house. The entire plot of land is exposed to the same environment and yet we will develop the idea of which part will become which room, depending on detailed specifics such as which side is north facing and which side is south facing. Which side of the plot gets the most light? Which side does the main rain and heavy winds come from? All these considerations, and others, about elements from the environment make us turn certain parts of the house into the hub of a specific activity or necessity. We create different rooms within the same house, each of these will hold different activities: the hallway, the sitting room, the dining room, the kitchen, the bathroom, the bedroom, and the storage room/pantry. Every one of the seven systems of a cell will be responsible for a specific activity, in the same way as each room in the house has a specific purpose in life.

The fixed part of the spectrum determines what species it will become and the basic structure that goes with it, but it is the influence of the environment that determines the ultimate physical manifestation of the captured energy. Once the structure has been completed, once the house has been built, it will operate specifically in the way it has been constructed. The kitchen may be very small and limited in cooking facilities. The bedroom may be spacious and full of light streaming in through large windows. The bathroom may be land locked within the building, without an outside window. Once the individual structure has been formed, this is who that individual is and how this specific life is going to operate. Of course, over time your idea about the house that you have built may change. Your needs may have changed. The times may also change, which means that the outside influences may be different, compared to those when the house was first built. They may have opened up a new busy road right on your doorstep. They may have chopped down the trees in the field behind your house, leaving you much more exposed to the elements. All of these changes, internally as well as externally, may make you wish your house had different qualities, was built differently, but essentially it is what it is. You may be able to make some alterations to the structure of the building, but the main alterations that you effectively can make are how you use the building that you are in. You can decide to use a room or part of a room for different purposes. You can decide to adjust the activities within a room to what the room can sustain rather than to what you would like it to be. You can decide to allocate some activities or part of some activities to a different location in the house. You can redecorate a room with a view to make it more functional, adjusted to the changed needs. All of this is exactly as it is in life. Once the individual organism has been fully formed, the basic structure is what it is, but we can learn to make some alterations in the way we occupy and live in that structure, rather than allowing a life style to continue within that structure, that will ultimately not be sustainable.

Conception

By the time mammals arrive on the evolutionary scene, the coming together of two separate sources of information as the basis for the creation of a new specimen has been well established. Male and female are two separate formats in which an individual can appear within a specific species. It requires the amalgamation of information from both sides of the species coin in the creative process of a new individual. Being members of the same species, almost their entire energetic background will be identical. They themselves having been formed in the same area – how else could they possibly meet up – means that the environmental influences that helped to shape them have been pretty similar, which means that they both, in their own way, have adjusted to similar outside stimuli, not exactly the same but similar. Hence, their entire energetic structure is going to be very compatible. The potential for development, held within this energetic structure, is pretty compatible, and the potential is, to a large degree, 'fixed' in the genetic part of their cells.

When the genetic information of the male specimen reaches the female and merges with it - in humans, one sperm enters the female egg cell – a new cell is formed, the first cell of the new specimen, the offspring of both parents. Nice. Except they forget to tell us how this new cell is being formed. What exactly happens? How do two DNA strains, that are not the same (coming from two different individuals), merge to form a full set of genes, which will give rise to an entirely new specimen of the same species?

Well there is a bit of magic happening here, and it all hinges on being male and female. Somehow, male and female are opposing poles in nature. They are not the same. They are opposites. These opposites can be observed quite easily within the nature of the women and the nature of the man, if we allow ourselves for a moment to let go of the idea that male and female must be the same. They are opposing poles. They have opposing polarities. You could say they contract and expand in an opposing fashion to one another. This creates movement and tension between the two. When the genetic information of one is coming in close contact with the genetic information of the other, in fact entering its space, the difference in electromagnetic potential, opposing poles, creates a spark, an electrical current that jolts the inert genes into movement. It links the two individual DNA strains together. Almost the entire length of the strains are identical as it contains the information about the species they both belong to, about the environment their ancestors have lived through and about the pedigree they each have. So these two DNA strains hold on to one another, intertwine and right before they close completely, the differences within the genetic makeup of these two specimens clash. Depending on the circumstances in which this joining together occurs, choices are being made with regards to either male or female information being included in the new DNA. The 'choices' are the result of the strength of the electromagnetic fields clashing. The circumstances, that provide the environment for this clash, are the personal energies both parents are manifesting at the time of the conception. Certain aspects of the female will be included and certain aspects of the male, but these will be definite choices of one or the other for every small aspect of the construction of the offspring. It will be either one or the other, never 'a combination', never a kind of compromise, of both parents.

Now the first cell, containing all the information about the construction of this new specimen, has been formed. Inside the mother's body, inside the mother's energy field, this new specimen of life will be formed. It takes ten to twelve weeks before the embryo takes on a human form. This is a remarkable observation. Looking more closely at every step of the development path towards that specific point, we notice something peculiar. The embryo quickly changes form. It takes on the shape of a bean, representing the plant stage, moving into a fish stage, an amphibian stage, a reptile stage, a bird stage and a mammal stage before arriving at a human form. These are exactly the different development stages the entire creation of life on earth has gone through, right up to this point. Weird, no? So, in the first ten to twelve weeks of the human foetal development the entire evolutionary process of life itself is being displayed, is being manifested. It is as if the specific human lifeform that is being created contains all the basic information about everything that was a precursor to that lifeform. More so, every human embryo displays exactly the same pathway and goes through exactly the same forms before arriving at the human form. Every time in the same way, irrespective of creed or colour of the human being in formation. There are no coloured human embryos! Furthermore, the embryonic development stages of a bird stop at the bird stage and do not contain a mammal form. The same is true for a salamander, which during its embryonic stages does not show a bird form or a mammal form. What is happening here? And where does the information for that process come from?

The only place it can come from is the genetic material inside that first cell. It is the genetic information that is being expressed. It turns out that scientists have calculated that during the entire lifespan of a human being only six percent of the entire DNA code is being used, is useful to sustain and to manage life. So much so that they even labelled the rest – 94% - of the human DNA as 'junk DNA'. Stuff we don't actually need in order to live. Maybe so, but now we see that all of that information is needed in order to be able to produce the human lifeform in the first place. The cells go through the entire production process to arrive at the right shape for that specific species. This entire process is driven from the inside out. It is an automatic process and nothing can interfere with it. The only thing that will stop it is when there is a fault in the genetic sequencing that should lead up to that human form. If somewhere on the way to the human form a major mistake has occurred in the assembly of the DNA information within that first cell, then the entire process will automatically be discontinued, and an early spontaneous abortion will take place, sometimes even before the women is fully aware that she is pregnant. Hence, the first ten to twelve weeks of the foetal development happen independently from the environment it finds itself in. Of course, when the mother kills herself the foetus dies too, but other than that, it doesn't bother the embryo at this stage what its outer-environment looks like or what it has to offer. At this stage, it requires nothing from its environment, apart from energies of life flowing by and holding this developing new life. The process is protected by the mother and carried by steady surroundings of a constant temperature and a constant water supply. But that is all that is required at this very early stage of the pregnancy. This is, of course, in total contrast to what the medical profession tells us. This information clearly indicates that it doesn't matter that in this very early stage of pregnancy the mother may be smoking, drinking alcohol or doing drugs. The expression of lifeforms of the different stages of the evolution within the embryonic development happens spontaneously and independently of its environment.

We have now reached the stage at which the human form has been completed. The features of this form will already hold information and adaptation relating to the tribe of humans this new specimen belongs to. In other words, specific features that will identify the person as an Asian person or an African person are already present. Furthermore, there will be indications of which part of the tribe the specimen belongs to. Besides obviously being Indian, this specimen may have features that relate specifically to Indian people who live at high altitude. All these elements relate to specific characteristics that belong to specific groups of people, living in specific circumstances on earth. Once we have established to which population group the new specimen belongs to and to which specific tribe he belongs to, we are ready for the further development of the individual. But before we do, let's take a closer look at the seed of life and what happens to it when life emerges from it.

The seed

The seed can be defined as 'a small object produced by a plant from which a new plant can grow' or in more general terms 'the beginning of something which continues to develop or grow'. The actual size of a plant seed does not give you any information about how large or small the plant that grows from it will be. A plant seed holds the potential to grow into a mature plant, capable of reproducing and creating new seeds. This means that all information that is required for the plant to become a fully mature plant is embedded within the tiny seed of the plant. It holds the potential. It doesn't guarantee a fully mature plant. For that to happen other supporting conditions need to be fulfilled. But what we can say is that the necessary information for that development is condensed, compressed within the space of the seed. The seed is, in other words, the most condensed part of the plant, taking up as little space as is possible without losing or deforming the information. This means that compressing the seed any further would destroy, break down, the stored information within it. Breaking open the seed doesn't give you access to the information held within.

Another interesting aspect of a seed is the fact that it hardly requires anything in order 'to survive' for an extended period of time. The oldest viable seed that has grown into a full plant was a roughly 2,000-year-old Judean date palm seed, recovered during excavations at Herod the Great's palace on Masada. It had been preserved in a cool, dry place, not by freezing. It was germinated in 2005. It stayed unaffected for over 2,000 years and was still able to manifest its potential, because all that time it was in a cool and dry place. For a plant seed 'to germinate', to come to life, it is said that three essential components are needed: soil, water, and sunlight. This is incorrect. No soil is needed to start the germination process. What is required is water and warmth. Inside the seed the conditions are dry and cool. When this meets outside conditions of moisture and warmth an electromagnetic potential is being created between the cold place and the warm place. This creates a flow of energy from cold to warm, from the inside out. The shell that protects the inside of the seed cracks and moisture flows in the opposite direction, from the outside environment into the seed, thereby ensuring a further swelling of the inner structure of the seed. This allows the tightly packed, folded into codes, plant structure to unfold. It appears to us as if the seedling starts to grow, as it begins to occupy more and more outside space.

It is developing spontaneously into a tiny form of the plant it potentially can become, only on moisture and warmth. Once it has reached its final, be it very small, complete form, the seedling will die unless it can find stimulation, nourishment, in its environment. At this point, soil becomes an essential component of the growth and the development of the plant.

In the same way, a mammal 'seed' cell requires an electromagnetic potential to manifest across the cell for it to become activated, to start to live, to start to develop into the potential it is holding inside. This initial process happens without detailed interference from the outside. It only requires a very basic steady environment. For seedlings it is constant moisture and warmth. For mammal embryos, it is a constant temperature and the availability of water.

When all growth stems from one form of seed or another, it makes sense to assume that the universe, as a developing entity, also has emerged from, has broken out of, a seed. This would then have to be the seed produced by another developing entity, by another universe. Its most compacted form will need to be some sort of seed, which, given the right circumstances, will burst open and begin to occupy space around itself. Gradually it will display the potential that was held within the seed at the moment of the breakthrough, of the Big Bang, if you like. As evolution moves on, the universe is step by step manifesting all the information it carries inside itself. Having arrived at the human being stage of its evolution, it isn't quite done yet! But it would help humanity if we were able to understand that we are part of the manifestation of a potential that a much greater entity than ourselves is holding and manifesting. We are one of the products of that entity. We are not the creator of that entity. Humanity is the flower on the plant. It is not the entire plant and not the creator of the plant.

Once the formation process is completed, further growth and development happens according to very specific pathways and interaction patterns.

Chapter 3
Development of a Human Being

Once the seedling has reached its final stage, once the embryonic phase of the human development is completed, then the newly forming organism, be it plant, animal or human, requires stimulation, nourishment from its environment to complete its full potential. The further development into its final form, complete with all the characteristics of a fully grown specimen, is dependent upon the influences coming from its immediate environment. Those influences, that information, is encoded in vibrations, in energy frequencies.

As far as the human development into a new specimen is concerned, the embryonic phase is completed around ten or twelve weeks into the pregnancy. From then on the embryo becomes a foetus, as named by the medical profession. Hence, without admitting it in so many words, they do recognise that the development that occurs before the tenth/twelfth week is different from the one that happens later. The difference, as we now know, is that the early development is entirely guided and ruled by the internal structure of the seed, the fertilised egg, independent of its surroundings. That changes once the full form of the structure has been completed.

Once the human form of the developing human being has been established, the balance shifts to include influences from the surrounding area of the developing human being, of the foetus. As every physical expression is a manifestation of energy, the surrounding 'area' of the foetus is the energy field of the mother. The foetus is entirely encapsulated by the mother, thereby being fully exposed to the energies the mother displays, manifests and live by. Whoever the mother is as a person, whatever the living conditions of the mother, physical but more importantly mental, those are the influences that the foetus is exposed to. That is the only 'picture' the foetus has of the outside world, the world that is waiting for it. This outside world may feel terrifying, or warm and friendly. But most aspects of that outside world will be noticed by the foetus and it will learn to link certain energetic changes within the field of the mother to changes that are happening around her. The further world, the greater universe (from the foetus' point of view), is experienced through the reaction pattern of the mother. The foetus does not need to know what exactly it is that is heading its way, it only needs to recognise the early signs and respond to it the way mother does. 'Why' is not important, just do it. It is 'the' way to survive. Because I, your mother, tell you so, show you so.

Through the teachings of its mother, the growing foetus learns about the kind of energetic environment it is going to encounter once it enters its outside world. Being embedded in the energy field of the mother, the foetus is sensitive to every slight alteration to that field. It learns to recognise the alterations and the circumstances in which they happen. That way it learns which reaction pattern belongs to what circumstances. It tries to copy the reaction pattern of the mother as it is the only coping mechanism that it is available to the foetus. Every set of circumstances has a specific reactive pattern attached to it. Learn from someone who has already done it!

There is, however, one other thing to consider with regard to this learning process. The foetus, the fully developed embryo, is constructed out of features that correspond to the female contribution of the building blocks and features that correspond to the male building blocks. No matter how compatible the parents may be in their way of reasoning, in judging the world and life, in the background of their upbringing, differences in some of the fundamental structures between them will always exist. This means that the foetus will not, on all points, on all characteristics, have a compatible nature to its mother. As a result, some of the reaction patterns the mother is displaying are either very difficult for the foetus to copy, draining a lot of energy and providing only a fragile balance, or even impossible to achieve. While in the first scenario, the foetus may do its level best to follow mother's lead, thereby forcing itself in a pattern that is not naturally its own, the situation in the second scenario is completely different. Here, the foetus will not, cannot, is unable, to follow mother's lead and it 'knows' it. Hence, the only option open to the foetus is to do the opposite. It does not possess the capacity to rationally analyse the situation and to find a compromise. The only thing that can be done is to refuse to follow suit. When mother, in response to a threatening outside situation, becomes submissive, the foetus may not be able to find that compatible with its own inner structure and may refuse to fold. When this is a repeated pattern, the foetus eventually will drift into anger, fuelled by the disturbing influence of the mother. The foetus is exposed to the influence of the energy field of the mother, not to the danger the mother perceives she is exposed to. When the mother keeps 'annoying' the foetus that way, keeps increasing the pressure on the foetus to force it into a reaction pattern it is unable to follow, the foetus will 'weaponise' itself against the mother on this aspect of life. It will respond by retreating away from how the mother is responding, which means that the reaction pattern of the foetus is going in the opposite direction. So when the mother becomes passive and submissive, the foetus will become aggressive and angry.

The reaction pattern the foetus learns and adopts is ultimately the result of the interaction between the energies in the outside field and the energies in the inside field. This is a universal law of nature. In the case of a developing foetus, the development of the human being is the result of the interaction between what it is surrounded by, the mother, and what its own structure is, its own makeup. From within the basic energetic balance of the foetus, it responds to the changing pressures that influence its own energy field. These interactions will result in reaction patterns that will form the basis of how this new human specimen is going to respond to the world it will enter once it is born. And remember that in order for a structure, inclusive a life structure, to be maintained as an entity, the internal balance of energies has to be respected. There is only a limited flexibility, a limited shift that can be allowed, before the structure will cease to be.

In music, harmony occurs when two or more notes are played simultaneously or consecutively. It is the way different pitches and chords are combined to create a sense of unity. The opposite, disharmony, is defined as a lack of agreement that often causes unhappiness or trouble. However, what would it mean for the energies within a field to be in perfect harmony?

Perfection is the way to stop everything. This happens when all parts of the world, the universe, and everything in general are in such a state that none of them want to change their state because each is in perfection. When things are in total perfect state, it also means that they are dead, that there is no more life, no more energy moving through them, because there is no movement. So maybe we need to take a different look at perfection. 'Perfection is an opportunity to constantly feel that you are able to move towards harmony.' Ideal harmony on its own is unattainable; it means the end of everything, the freezing of the universe if we can imagine it that way. Therefore to us, perfection lies in the fact that we can move towards such harmony. Maybe we need to see perfection, like everything else in life, as a journey, as a learning process. Maybe growing up, developing, is all a process of moving towards that 'perfect' inner balanced state, inner harmony. It is the moving towards it, rather than the attainment of it, that is perfection in life, and not the absolute perfection itself as life would be extinguished by the perfection itself.

We can now confidently state that at every moment in time the entire universe is in harmony, is in balance. This means that, at every moment in time, all internal reactions are what they should be and everything that is manifesting is the only thing it can be, given the specific circumstances of that moment. In other words, perfect balance. However, every moment in time is different. When we look at this internal balance of the universe, we observe that the balance shifts all the time. So it is perfect as it is, right now, and it changes to perfection as it is a moment later. When that internal movement stops, life disappears out of the universe, evolution stops and nothing will be created anymore. How does this affect the foetus?

The foetus is trying to move towards a 'liveable' balance, an inner harmony, by moving towards it. In the first place, the foetus can only accept what someone else tells it. The foetus takes on board the information it learns from someone else and, for most part, adopts it. On certain aspects of life, it turns out that this is not an option for the specific foetus in question, so it moves away from it. The foetus is a sponge for information, but with a hard core, with limitations, from which it will bounce back. It sucks up the information and its physical form enlarges, well adapted to be able to manifest the required reaction patterns. When the baby is born and enters the world as a separate entity, it is equipped with an inner foundation, which is grounded in human history, in tribal and family knowledge, and with a set of automated reaction patterns that will navigate it through the changing energies of the world it will encounter. This set of reaction patterns will ensure the survival of the new human specimen within the circumstances of that specific life.

Matter is created in three steps, moving from light matter to compact matter: gas, liquid and solid. In mammals, to which human beings belong, life is created in three steps, from compact to light. The seed and subsequent formation of the species form of the particular specimen is followed by the installation of automated reaction patterns which will provide the specimen with survival skills. Once the specimen is directly confronted with the outside world it learns behavioural skills and techniques from its fellows, which allows for choices to be made in life. Hence, three layers of development: physical format, automated survival skills, and living skills. From most physical to nonmatter as in behaviour skills.

This third stage of building a new human being begins at birth. We call the years to come 'the formative years' of the child. As we have seen, this is incorrect as there are two formation stages prior to this one, but we tend to view the arrival of a new baby as the start of a new life, thereby ignoring the fact that this life started quite a while back, in different circumstances, in a different environment. A new born baby is not a blank page. It already has experiences and skills on how to deal with the life. It can no longer be moulded into just about anything. It already has its specifics such as its limitations, its weak points and its strong points. It already has its talents. It is this background that the baby brings into the world, the world that we know and reside in.

The baby has been preparing for this transition by 'listening' to its mother. It is taking mothers' lead on how to navigate through the obstacles of living in the world. One could say that the baby is hiding behind a mummy skirt. Now that the baby has arrived in the world, it is meeting all the energies directly. It is, however, recognising quite a number of them through the reaction patterns of the mother, and this is, for the most part, confirmed by direct observation and the sensing of the mother in the world itself. The baby, in the first place, will be testing out what it has been taught in the womb school of life. It is looking for conformation of the reaction patterns it has adopted from its mother. And mostly it will find that conformation. In a dramatic twist, it may turn out that the fear mother is displaying, say for instances for her partner, is way out of proportion with reality - a paranoid idea of being in constant danger from her partner - and this may be something the baby quickly picks up, which will allow it to change its own reaction pattern towards its father, from being fearful to a more relaxed state. But on the whole, the reaction patterns of the mother point in the right direction and the baby is able to check these out and establish these patterns as being correct, useful and necessary, even if they don't easily fit into the internal structure of the baby.

Being in direct contact with the world, the new specimen is now in a position to create its own experiences and build its own relationship with the outside world. However, we should never lose sight of the fact that it cannot escape the walls that are already in existence around that specific life. There are the limitations linked to the history of the tribe and the family, which are further streamlined by the choices of reaction patterns, aimed at its survival, and with the mother as the supplier. With this knowledge in its backpack, the new specimen takes its first careful steps into the world. It will approach the world from what it already 'knows' about it, and it will place its own experiences into that framework. Every experience will get a place in its memory bank. Every experience will be filed somewhere in this cabinet. However, what this cabinet looks like, how many draws there are, how many locked cupboards and how many open shelves, depends on what went before. The construction of this filing cabinet depends on information from tribe and family and on the learned need for specific filing space, which comes through the information the foetus received from its mother.

The growing child initially takes on board everything it comes across as true. It has no databank to question or challenge anything. Everything is seen as real. Everything is filed 'as is'. At least for as long as there is appropriate space in the filing cabinet. Gradually, as the child is getting a bit older, it learns to be more careful. However, being able to question your own observation or a statement made about an observation requires access to different information. Somewhere in the child databank there should be some stored information that does not correspond to what it is currently being confronted with. Not only should this 'different' information exist within its databank, the child should also have a recollection of that existence. Somehow it should 'sense' that this isn't quite correct, that there may be the potential of a different truth. Depending on whether the child, by its environment, is allowed to question the authority of the more experienced members of its world or not will allow or restrict the development of critical skills within the child.

Becoming a young adult, the new specimen is now equipped in a very specific way to continue its journey through life. It has an internal information source that has been stocked with ancient general information, with more specific information from a personal nature and with wider, more diverse, information from 'the world'. Now the young adult enters the world completely by himself, becoming exposed directly to the influences of the big world. Armed with his set of reaction patterns, with his belief systems and his judgements, he faces the full impact of the world on his own personal life.

One can only approach life and experiences with the knowledge one holds. There is no other way. What you think is right, is what you will strive for. But we all have a different set of 'know-how's' that we bring to this world. What is perceived as 'right' or as 'true' by one person may be totally different to another. It all depends on what is stored in your knowledge cupboard. However, every individual will have no choice but to face life, armed with his own 'right' and his own 'truth'.

The young adult is faced with difficulties in life. He knows what to do about it, because he has answers in his information storage cupboard. He uses these answers and expects the problems to be solved. And when it appears that way, so far so good. Conformation that we are right and that we can continue as we are doing. But, as time goes by, as more and more experiences repeat themselves in a slightly different fashion, he begins to notice that the preformulated answers are no longer having a positive impact on the situation. Life, bit by bit, gets out of sink. He struggles to maintain his balance. He wobbles. He nearly falls over.

Life expresses a sense of imbalance in several possible ways, depending on which type of energy is being put under the most pressure. We may display physical discomfort or definite illnesses, no longer physically functioning properly. We may become aware that our mind is no longer capable of providing us with a way out of trouble. A sense of mental imbalance may become noticeable. Or we may simply find that no matter how hard we try to achieve something specific in life, it is not coming to fruition. All our efforts get blocked. There is no way forward in the direction we are wanting to go. All of these could be indications that the automated approach to life, the learned foundation of 'right' and 'true' may no longer be appropriate.

The now not so young adult has the opportunity to learn his own, very new, lessons of life. He experiences what works for him and what doesn't. Using his unconscious automatic reaction pattern arsenal will deliver results, or should we say 'responses'. Certain circumstances arise and he reacts to those in the manner he has learned. He is not aware of the process that results in his response, but if he wants to, he can become aware of the fact that his response, although entirely logical and normal to him, is only one possible response out of a multitude of possibilities. The world, his surroundings, will now react to his response and this is an opportunity to truly evaluate how effective and efficient his automatic responses still are in his life. If the reaction his response is triggering becomes more and more obstructive in a specific situation, an alert individual may begin to question what he is doing himself, rather than continuing to blame the rest of the world for being 'wrong'. This is an opportunity to question ones' own evaluation system, the system of true and false that one has put together in the early days of ones' life. Why is this important?

In everything is evolution. Nothing stands still, remember? So, the universe is changing. The earth is changing. Human society is changing. All of this means that how we used to do things in the past will, at some point, become inadequate. Our reaction pattern, based on what human beings have learned, will at some point need a revision. What we have considered to be true may, at some point, be shown to us as 'not true'. It is the point of learning something new, of taking another step towards the truth, towards perfection, towards harmony. Each individual, later on in life, will be confronted with signs that his reaction is no longer producing the desired, the expected, effect. It is nothing less than an invitation of the universe to take a step forward, to add your step to the evolution of knowledge.

This is how one remains in balance! We have to learn to move on. Holding on to established routines, to proven ideas of 'good' and 'truth', will bring us out of sink with our surroundings, our world, our universe. Staying in balance requires an internal shift, away from our established convictions. But what do they have to turn into?

We learn through observation. As a foetus and a very young child, we learned from observing others, their behaviour, their reasoning, their convictions. Later on, as a young adult we learned from observing what others, regarded as experts, point out that lies ahead of us. Now we have the opportunity to learn from what the universe shows us what works and what doesn't. The problem for most individuals is the restriction they feel from being unfaithful to their old beliefs, and in many instances also being unfaithful to what people around them still want to hold on to. Having to admit to oneself that the world isn't what you thought it was, that the solutions you believed in are not what they promised to be, and that not making this switch will end your life as you have known it, becomes the crossroads of life. Of course, the truth is that the life that you have known has already ended, since your old reaction pattern is no longer effective in producing the outcome you require, which means that the true choice in front of you is in fact one of personal survival. Either you change to restore harmony with your environment or you remain out of balance. This gap between where you are and where the balance point is will only increase over time. Remember, nothing stays the same. If the gap isn't closing, it will open up even further. And the only way you are closing the gap is by doing things differently in your life, as the routine you have used is responsible for the occurrence of the gap in the first place. You may find that making different choices in life is extremely difficult for you, but it would be good to remember that not making different choices means that your life is on its way out, as a result of this specific situation.

Making the conscious choice not to change – being aware of the choices in front of you and deciding not to change – will bring peace of mind to your life. You will understand that your life is out of balance and that you have decided to keep it that way, in which case you no longer have to worry about any physical or mental expression of this imbalance. Whatever happens to you and to your health, you will know that it is a result of the choice you have made. You are at peace with your decision and you allow life to slowly retreat from the incarnation that you are. There are no good or bad choices. The good or bad only lies in the reaction of your fundamental self upon your choices. If your 'soul' is not in alignment with your choices, you will not find peace of mind, you will continue to be at war with the choices you are making in the outside world. You will experience this internal fight as a feeling of having made 'a bad choice'. As far as the universe and creation is concerned, every natural reaction is the 'right' one in order to either restore the balance or to elicit moving into a new balance. Either it is conservative good or it is progressive good.

Life is indeed this balanced journey towards more insight and more knowledge, delivered by the universe, by life itself, by nature. Every single human life is about learning a specific aspect of life, of nature, to add to the pool of insight and of knowledge that humanity is holding. Every single human life will move it a little bit further along this road, even if we are unaware of this. Every single human life is a grain of sand, consolidated energy, which contributes to the entire beach of knowledge about life and nature. As such, the single grain of sand doesn't mean much, has no value, and yet, without it there would be no larger picture. Without it, there could not be a beach, made up of grains of sand.

Every human life is transient, is a mere spec in time. It means nothing. But without it, the universe would not be able to evolve any further. The purpose of one human life is not to impress other human lives, is not to be an example to be copied by others. The purpose of one human life is to find its own, over time shifting, balance and to follow that shifting for as long as is sustainable for that one life. It is not a place in human history that counts. It is a place in the evolution of the universe that truly counts and that place is secured from the moment the embryo becomes a foetus, from the moment a human form adds its weight to the pool of humanity. And every experience adds to the pool of knowledge the universe is gathering.

So there is no need for an individual to try and please his fellow men. The more that individual succeeds in pleasing his own inner fundamental structure, the greater his contribution towards the growth and development of the universe will be. But don't worry as every small bit helps.

Chapter 4

The Functioning of Life

All matter, including all living matter, is a condensation of small parts of the energy field. The energy field that holds everything is the universe, which is a 'balloon' in which moving energy waves are creating space. The movement of the various energies inside the universe is caused by local differences in electromagnetic potential, in turn caused by differences in pressure and temperature. You can visualise this by looking at weather patterns on earth, where the constant movement of air also keeps the atmosphere in its place and ensures that it neither collapses onto the earths' surface or drifts off into space.

In certain parts of the universal field, the contraction of energies restricts its movement and we perceive those areas as clouds of gas. Inside these clouds, small areas contract even further producing liquid clouds. In some parts these contract even further and become solid matter. After some time, the pressure on the liquid cloud keeps condensing the material structures more and more until a very particular configuration of material bits results in the formation of a cell, which now, under the pressure expands rather than contracts. So, inside the liquid field and connected to the solid field, life emerges in very specific circumstances, which occurs in only very specific and tiny places within the entire universal field, and only after a very long development, creating the exact circumstances for cells to form.

The structure of life is energetic, and the material expression within that structure will change when the balance of energies of that part of the spectrum, that is being expressed, changes. The physical structure of living organisms is a direct expression of the energetic spectrum it represents. The physical structure of living organisms doesn't have an existence without the energies out of which the organisms emerge. The specific format and the specific characteristics of a living organism is a direct expression of its own specific energies, the energies that surround the hard core physical matter, energies in which the living organism bathes.

How do changes in energy frequency, amplitude, speed and so on translate into the material living organism? What is 'living'? How does a living organism function?

Whatever we are talking about with regards to the universe and energies, you should always bear in mind that everything has to stay in balance. Hence, whatever the physical state or the functionality of a living organism might be, we should always remember that it is in balance. What nature shows us is the truth. Natural phenomena don't cheat. They don't play tricks. It is what it is, even if we fail to understand 'why'.

Transforming moving energy into fixed energy, using some of the energy to put into matter, indicates the two basic forms living energy is presenting to us. When energy is free to move and can freely adjust to changing circumstances it is called *kinetic energy*. When energy is very limited in its range and is stuck, as is the case in matter, we are going to call it *matter energy*. The matter energy is basically condensed, compacted, kinetic energy. The structure of a living organism, therefore, is matter energy, a transformation from kinetic energy. It is a balanced expression of the kinetic energy spectrum that compacts into this particular physical form. Part of the energy that creates the living organism still remains as kinetic energy, moving around, in the vicinity of, the physical structure of the organism and as it were, is stuck to the physical part of that energy field. The body of the organism is made up of a number of cells and of space in between cells. It has a material structure of sugars, fats, proteins and so on, which is matter energy, but there is also movement within this physical structure, which is internal kinetic energy. The outer kinetic energy is responsible for the movement the organism makes in the outside world. As far as plants are concerned, this is very limited and can be described as waving in the wind. The inner kinetic energy is responsible for the movement of internal energies, which is communication that is needed to maintain the inner balance, to keep all inner structures 'in line'. Creating living physical matter also creates an internal space, because living organisms 'grow' into the outer world, occupying more and more outer space, making that space energetically 'their own'. That space, which was part of the open outer space within the field, has now been changed to a new area of space inside the matter. And as every space within the universe is filled with energy, it shouldn't surprise us that we find kinetic energy inside matter energy.

All energy is part of an energy scale or a spectrum, in which we can recognise parts, sections, portions, but they all remain connected. If one part of the spectrum contracts, it lengthens other parts within the spectrum as the entire spectrum has to be filled at all times. And as we have seen, it is this contracting and expanding that causes the entire field to have an internal movement. This is true within the space of the universe as it is true within the space of a living organism. In fact, this internal movement is the reason why we call that part of the physical universe 'living'. And what is responsible for the internal movement of energies?

One cell, the very basic structure of life, is constructed out of seven different systems, as is the case for any organism. Different systems mean that the energies that are being expressed in these seven specific ways are different in their composition. We have already mentioned that they are all made up from the same seven tissues, so the differences within the systems don't come from different building blocks. Indeed, the building blocks, and consequently the energies that created these building blocks, are all the same, however, the specific combination of these energies in the various tissues and in the various systems is different each time. The same note in different octaves. The same energy at different levels. And combining these notes in different compositions create different songs, all made up from the same notes. These differences in the same energy, in close proximity of each other, create slight electromagnetic potentials, which create small currents between them. Now we have movement inside the cell, inside a system and between the various systems. These movements are all movements towards perfection. The aim is to equalise the electromagnetic potentials, but because of the state of flux the universe and the creation is in, that goal will never be reached.

So there is constant movement in the inner space of the organism, which means that there is constant change. The balance of potentials between the various parts of the construction is constantly changing. This results, in part, in the growth process we observe in every living creature from birth onwards, and which will keep on going into what we call old age and eventually death. It is a natural process to grow and develop and then become old and deteriorate towards a failing of the system, towards a breaking up of the balance, of the harmony. Hence, the balance in that specific life changes all the time, simply because there is constant internal movement of energy. But that is not all.

As the entire universe is a constantly moving energy field, the field that a living organism is part of is also constantly on the move. So, the field from which the individual organism originates is constantly shifting its balance too. Let's see if we can paint a clear picture of what energetic structure we are actually talking about. From the inside out, there is internal kinetic energy, surrounded by matter energy, surrounded by the kinetic energy that created that matter. That kinetic energy is part of the kinetic energy field of the species the said organism belongs to and which contains billions of individual specimens. More specifically, we have the internal energy of a human being, the physical body of the human being and the individual energy field of that individual, which is part of the human energy field itself. The human energy field is divided into fields of energy where the balance is different, still human but differently human. There are separations within the human field that give rise to the various human races, being different in structure and in characteristics. The entire human field is part of the energetic field of mammals, which in turn is part of the entire animal field, which is part of the field of living organisms, that was created from a specific set of energies within the liquid cloud field, which is part of the gas cloud field within the universal field. And all these fields have movement. And none of these fields remain the same. But if a change happens in an outer field then there has to be a response in the inner field in order to keep the balance. So now we also have movement across the fields too and these are instigated by indirect interferences. Think about a glass table top with a magnet lying on the top of it and you holding a magnet underneath the glass. When you move your hand, the magnet on top of the glass will move too. That is how movement in the outside field creates a response movement on the inside.

How can we, with this knowledge, explain how the matter energy changes over time? What exactly is happening for matter to be changed into something we may call an illness or an imbalance?

There is a harmony inside an energy field and the energy field is drawn to maintaining this harmony. This is why it shifts all the time in order 'to keep things together'. An energy field with physical matter is no different. This means that there is a natural tendency for the matter to keep itself together, to maintain the harmony within that part of the spectrum that is expressed in matter. Hence, living matter, every living organism, has a natural tendency to keep itself together, alive if you like. It will continuously be drawn towards its inner harmony. And even though the balance of that harmony is shifting over time, at any given moment in time it is harmonious inside the organism. So, the energy flowing inside a person is in balance, is the best way to maintain life at that point in time. The inner energy flow and the outer energy flow of the organism are also in balance with each other at any given moment in time. They are both part of the same energy field, the energy of that individual. The physical manifestation of that individual is sandwiched between those two energy compartments, and since these are in balance with one another the physical manifestation is also always in balance and an exact and correct manifestation of the balance within the energy field. Whatever the physical matter is expressing, it is always a clear and precise manifestation of the balance within its entire energetic field. If you find that the physical balance in life is stretched and difficult to maintain – you are feeling 'under the weather', feeling ill – it is due to a high pressure on some energies within your personal field.

Over time, the balance of your personal energy field changes all the time. If you doubt that, I suggest you take out a photo album and have a look at pictures of yourself as a baby, as a child, as a teenager and as a young adult. It must be obvious that pictures, taken at different times, show a different person each time. You may recognise certain features but much has changed in the physical appearance. And the same is true if we were to recall how that individual behaved over time. So, the question is: 'what is driving these physical changes?'

It must be energy! It can't be anything else, but how does it do it? The balance of energies that make up the field is constantly shifting. Those parts of the energy spectrum within the field that are manifested in matter will consequently change too. How does the material expression of an individual human being change over time? Well, the inner field is directly connected, is part of the outer field of the person and this outer field is part of a humanity field. It interfaces with the energy fields of other individuals, of other lives that intertwine.

So when there is a shift in balance amongst those lives, the life of the individual, and consequently the physical matter of that individual, changes with it. The lives, and energy fields, of all those lives closely connected to the life of the individual are all part of larger fields that eventually hold all human lives. And this field in turn is part of the mammal energy field, which is part of the animal field, which is part of the natural world on earth. And earth is part of the physical material, produced within the universal field. All of these fields internally move. You can imagine that a field within a field may be pressurised in parts by its mother field. This, in turn, will respond to the increased pressure by contracting in certain parts, which then in turn will pressurise parts of a field that lies within that field, and so on. This very much looks like the changes that occur within one field are mainly driven by the energy flow and the changes that occur in the outer fields. And that makes sense too, because that way the main changes, the more permanent long term changes, within all the fields scattered within the universal field are all part of one and the same evolution. It is all an expression of how the universal field moves forward in balance, in harmony. Whatever internal changes may take place, they will be overridden and steered by changes in the surrounding field. This means that changes within nature, which are instigated by changes within the universal balance, will direct balanced responses within the field of humanity. Changes within human beings in general – in knowledge (rationality, thinking), in sensing (emotions, feeling), in belief systems – will drive changes within the race fields of humanity and that will have a changing effect upon the energy field of the individuals within those groups. The individual energy field will then express those changes in the physical matter of the individual. It all follows one line of development. It all goes where the universe is going in terms of evolution, in terms of development. And all the way through these changes, there will be harmony within the fields. There will be a balance of energies.

Energy interferences

In physics, interference is a phenomenon in which two coherent waves are combined by adding their intensities or displacements with due consideration for their phase difference. The resultant wave may have greater amplitude (constructive interference) or lower amplitude (destructive interference) if the two waves are in phase or out of phase, respectively. Interference effects can be observed with all types of waves. The principle of superposition of waves states that when two or more propagating waves of the same type are incident on the same point, the resultant amplitude at that point is equal to the vector sum of the amplitudes of the individual waves.

Coherent waves are waves that maintain a constant phase difference and have the same frequency. This means their oscillations are synchronised, allowing them to interfere predictably, creating patterns of constructive and destructive interference. For an interference pattern to be observable over any extended period of time, the two sources of light must be coherent with respect to each other. This means that the light sources must maintain a constant phase relationship. However, most light sources do not emit true harmonic waves; instead, they emit waves that undergo random phase changes millions of times per second. Such light is called incoherent. Interference still occurs when light waves from two incoherent sources overlap in space, but the interference pattern fluctuates randomly as the phases of the waves shift randomly. Detectors of light, including the eye, cannot register the quickly shifting interference patterns, and only a time-averaged intensity is observed. So we only observe interference patterns of coherent waves, even though noncoherent waves also have an interference pattern, albeit not a constant one. Any detector of light must have a fixed range it is looking for. So only coherent waves within that range can be observed. All physical expressions, from light to sound to solid matter, are expressions of coherent wave interferences. Because matter is an energy spectrum, fixed as a result of consistent pressure on the energy field, the only energy interference that is possibly going to create a change in the form and/or function of the physical live form is a coherent interference.

Waves of the same frequency with a constant phase difference are basically 'the same notes in different octaves'. It is the colour red within every one of the seven colours of the visible light spectrum. Hence, the energy combination that creates one particular tissue of the body, as we have mentioned in a previous chapter, is essentially the same energy combination, albeit in a different phase, as the one that manifests as one particular system of the body. As we now have seven main notes, energy groups, linked to seven main tissues and seven main systems, we might as well connect them by an identical 'energy phase number'. Ignore why these are not in numerical order when you go down the list. The explanation for this, you can find in the book *'Why Me? – Science and Spirituality as inevitable bed partners'* (ISBN-13:9789082785425) by Dr Patrick Quanten & Erik Bualda.

1	water/skin tissue	lymphatic system
4	blood tissue	circulatory system
6	muscle tissue	digestive/respiratory system
2	fat tissue	mobility system
5	bone tissue	sensory system
7	nervous tissue	nervous system
3	reproductive tissue	glandular system

We can now see that when energy phase 1 changes even one of its characteristics, it will have an effect on the water/skin tissue, which is used in all systems, but not in the same amount in each of these systems, as it will also have a serious effect on the balance within the entire lymphatic system. It is only changes in the wave property of one energy phase that will affect all parts of the living organism, albeit not to the same extent. The more of this energy phase that is part of the build-up of the structure, the greater the impact. For instance, there is a lot of muscle tissue in the digestive system, so a change in energy phase 6 may well affect the function of the digestive system, in the first instance, and maybe later on even the structure of the digestive system, but it may also be noticed within the mobility system as there too is a lot of muscle tissue present. There is a high percentage of nervous tissue within the nervous system, but also within the sensory system.

The main properties of waves, and these are all subject to potential change, are as follows:

• Amplitude: The maximum displacement of the wave from the mean position is called the amplitude of the wave. It is the maximum height from the centre line to the crest or the trough. The crest is the highest point of the wave and the trough is the lowest point of the wave. Amplitude is measured in metres.

• Frequency: The number of vibrations passing a fixed point in a given amount of time is called frequency. The unit of frequency is Hertz.

- Wavelength: Wavelength is the distance between two identical points (adjacent crests or troughs). It is measured in metres. Frequency and wavelength are inversely proportional to each other.
- Time Period: The time taken by a complete wave to pass through a particular point in space is called the time period. The time period is measured in seconds. The time period is the reciprocal of the frequency.
- Speed: For a wave, speed is the distance travelled by a particular point on the wave in the given interval of time. Speed is measured in metres per second.
- When we talk about the waves in creation, the entire electromagnetic (EM) wave spectrum, we should be aware of the specific characteristics of electromagnetic waves.
- They do not require a medium for propagation. They can travel through a vacuum, like outer space, unlike mechanical waves (like sound waves) which need a medium (like air or water) to travel. This is because EM waves are disturbances in electric and magnetic fields, which can exist and propagate even in the absence of matter.
- EM waves are transverse in nature. This means that the electric and magnetic fields within the wave oscillate perpendicular to the direction the wave is travelling in. In simpler terms, imagine holding a rope and shaking it up and down; the wave travels along the rope, but the movement of the rope (and thus the wave) is perpendicular to the direction the wave is going. This is analogous to how EM waves behave.
- They are not deflected by electric and magnetic fields.
- EM waves get polarised. Polarisation refers to the direction of the electric field vector as the wave propagates. In an unpolarised EM wave, the electric field oscillates in all directions perpendicular to the direction of propagation. However, when an EM wave is polarised, the electric field oscillates in a specific direction.
- They carry energy and momentum. This momentum is transferred to charged particles or objects when they interact with the wave. This momentum transfer can result in various effects, including:
  - Radiation pressure: The momentum transfer from electromagnetic waves to a surface results in radiation pressure.
  - Particle acceleration: Electromagnetic waves can accelerate charged particles to high energies.

In short, electromagnetic waves can change in amplitude, in frequency and wavelength, in speed, and in direction of travel. They transfer their energy onto the matter they encounter, or the matter within the field that they travel in, by putting pressure on the outside of the field that has the matter at its centre, and/or by accelerating the speed of the small particles that make up that matter. Pressure results in an initial effect of compressing the field matter and increasing the internal vibration of matter, the internal speed of energy flow in matter, which creates extra heat and extra pressure on the existing internal balance of matter. Accelerating the speed of small particles within the field increases movement, resistance to movement and consequently heat. So, what changes the function and/or the structure of physical matter? Pressure onto the field of the matter and increased temperature of the field of the matter.

Is it possible for us to recognise what has changed within the EM wave through our limited observation powers? Well, there are some things we can consider. Amplitude indicates the 'loudness' of the information carried by the wave. The higher the wave energy is, the more powerful the information is being experienced within the field and by everything it passes on its way. The frequency, and related to this the wavelength, indicates the kind of information the wave carries. Moving from one frequency to another changes the note in sound, changes the colour in vision. The speed a wave travels at shows how much time is left before that information reaches you. This may be important in the first place with regards to survival. Animals sense an impending grave danger such as a tsunami or a thunderstorm, which allows them time to get to safety. The direction of travel of a wave is also important to be able to judge properly as it gives you information about whether or not you will become exposed to it. It also directs you to a specific area in space where the source of this information is located. If the wave is passing you by without interference, there is nothing you need to do. All living creatures are equipped to sense changes within the field they are in and major changes in the field that surrounds them all. It is another indication of how everything is interconnected and how information, EM waves, are a shared feature of creation.

Functioning matter

Within the space of the living organism energy flows. Matter is the condensation of a limited number of waves, frequencies, of a small part of the spectrum. The waves, movement and information exchanges (wave interferences) within the limited range of the living organism is in balance, is harmonious. As we have seen, even without any specific outside interference, the internal balance within the organism doesn't remain the same. Energies move and interfere with one another, thereby exchanging information, which after a while even alters the functioning and later on the structure of the organism. All within the set limits of the harmonious set of octaves. That is one balance on the move.

The other one is the balance between that one living organism and its outside world. The organism has to be in balance, in harmony, with its surroundings. In nature, we see that conflicts, clashes, only last a very short period of time, and in between those fights and disagreements all organisms return to an inner status of calmness and harmony. There is no hatred or jealousy of envy or revenge. There is conflict, followed by a resolution. Everything is instantaneous, and that is why it is always in balance. The conflicts are balanced reactions back and forth. The resolution is the end of the movement of the conflict balance. There is balance in the conflict as all reactions are appropriate, and there is balance in the in-between periods as there is peace and harmony inside and all around.

However, at any given moment in time, the organism has to possess the possibility to respond to outside influences. In fact, at best it should be aware, ready to respond, even before the particular circumstance arises. It should know that a potential danger lurks around the corner, because waiting for the confrontation to happen, being surprised by the impending danger, seriously reduces the chances of survival. On the other hand, being constantly on the alert for potential danger only results in an extremely high consumption of energy and focuses life entirely on life outside of the organism, ignoring the inner requirements to allow the inner energies to flow smoothly, unpressurised.

Luckily, no animal has the capacity to imagine danger. When they sense 'potential' danger, it is because it is a real possibility, not an imagined possibility. Only human beings are smart enough to imagine pending danger without there being any real 'possible' danger. Only human beings are developed enough to override their natural sensitivity and replace natural sensitivity connection to the entire creation with rationality. No other part of creation has this rational 'sense'. Using this as our source of information for life, we disconnect ourselves from nature and from everything in it.

How does this sensing of the outside world work? Well, everything is made up from the same seven principle energy phases. So, whatever the physical matter of the organism is, it has been constructed with the same basic elements that its outside world has been constructed from. This means that the organism has a certain balanced connection with every bit of the outside world via its own physical matter. If a change occurs in one of the characteristics of the energy phase in the outside world, it will have an effect, however slight, on a part of the physical structure of the organism. So when some people proudly declare that 'they feel it in their water', or 'they feel it in their bones', they are not joking. This is real. This is how nature works, even if most of us have lost the conscious connection to this information. When the moon position in relation to earth changes, it has an effect on the energy field of nature and consequently of human beings.

For instance, if the amplitude of the energy phase in the outside world (the wave of attracting and requiring nourishment) increases as a result of a predator being in the neighbourhood, the organism senses this alteration. If the direction of the energy phase in the outside world (the wave scanning the environment for nourishment) changes and becomes more powerful and focused (like a laser light, lots of coherent waves), the organism senses this alteration. If the speed of travel of the energy phase in the outside world (the speed in which the predator moves through the area) increases, the organism senses this alteration. So there is an awareness of elements of the outside world, in particular those elements that have a possible impact on the inner workings of the specific organism. Becoming aware of specific alterations in the outside world makes the organism respond in the most appropriate way to the information gained. The energetic changes in the outside world trigger appropriately balanced changes, within the energies of the organism. Every internal system, and with it every type of tissue within every internal system, will alter its function appropriately, meaning in a coordinated, balanced, way. The information received does not have to be processed by a complex evaluation system before it can be used. It is a direct connection. Whatever energy in the outside world and in whatever manner that energy changes, it affects that specific energy inside the organism. And since every part of the organism is constructed with the same elements, all parts of the organism receive the message of change at the same time. Not in the same way, as not every part of the organism is constructed with the same combination of all building elements, but they all receive the message of change. The entire organism feels the message from the outside world and is, therefore, capable of responding in a coherent manner to it, in an instance.

If the change in the outside world has no particular meaning to a specific organism then it won't receive that message and it won't respond. For instance, when a predator arrives in a certain area and you are not its prey, your organism doesn't need to know that predator is nearby. The changes that have occurred in the outside world are not falling within the range of your species spectrum, which means that you do not 'sense' those changes, as you are not within reach of those frequencies. Think about it in terms of a dog's whistle. When someone blows the dog's whistle that signal does not enter your system. It reaches you, but there is no internal structure that 'resonates' with that specific frequency, with that specific information. If the information of the outside world does not enter your system, your system does not need to respond to it. Hence, there is a lot of truth (not fully, but a lot) in the saying 'what you don't know can't hurt you'.

Functioning human being

On a physical level, we now know how the communication between the energies in the outside world and those on the inside of an organism works. Every cell of every organism has on its surface, on its outer membrane, loads of small antennae sticking out into the outside world of the cell. Initially, researchers had the world convinced that these were receptors to which specific proteins, hormones and other transmitters could attach in order to deliver a message to the cell. The idea was that cells within the body structure communicated with each other through the release of physical matter, carried by the bloodstream. However, soon this theory was shown to fall short of providing answers with regards to the speed of certain physical responses, to the accuracy of responses and to the specificity of responses.

It turned out that these 'docking stations' were in fact tiny antennae. Each of these is sensitive to only one frequency. When that frequency is present in the vicinity of the cell, and this may be amongst other cells of the same organism or it may be in the outer environment of the organism itself, the antenna gets stimulated, activated. The antenna is connected to the inside of the cell and activation of the antenna sends an electrical impulse into the cell. To each of these specific impulses, trigged by a specific frequency, is a specific cellular response attached. When the signal reaches the inside of the cell, the cell always responds in the same way. The specific signal activates a specific pathway within the metabolism of the cell. When no signal is being picked up the cell does not produce that specific response. Every time the signals come in, the cell follows the same pathway, creates the same action, for instance produces the same molecule. It is an automatic response to an electromagnetic signal, picked up in the outside world.

Life communicates with the rest of creation, with other living creatures, with nature, on an energetic basis. Information is being exchanged via frequencies, wave interferences and corresponding actions are automatically activated. This indicates that all of nature and all of life is linked together and evolves, moves, in sink. Interconnectedness and total communication systems ensure a coordinated choreography of all of creation. Everything is in balance within the larger picture.

That is when all antennae cover the entire spectrum of possibilities that are potentially present in the outside world. But as living organisms have become more and more complex, a wider range of information is required in order to be able to maintain that harmony. In physical terms that means that an ever increasing number of antennae need to be placed on the surface of all cells of the more complex organisms. Human beings are the most complex structure within creation at this point in the evolutionary process.

The cells of human beings are also equipped with a large number of antennae. On the one hand, there are the permanent antennae, which are constantly listening out for specific frequencies. These are very much related to immediate survival information and rescue responses the organism should never have any doubt about. Besides those, there are also a number of antennae that can be deployed or can be folded up. When they stick out from the cell surface, the cell is potentially receiving that kind of information from its environment. When they are withdrawn, the cell becomes deaf to that specific frequency. This means that, even when the frequency is present in its environment, the cell will not be aware of it, will not send an activating signal into the cellular metabolism and will not, as a consequence, have a response ready. In this manner, the cell is incapable of responding to something it didn't hear, it wasn't aware of.

The truth is that we are unable to process all available information in the ether at the same time. Also, there is no requirement to have 'all' information as the only thing that is truly important is the information required for survival. With the organism becoming more complex in structure and functioning, it requires ever more information, from an ever widening spectrum, in order to maintain that all important balance as more and more factors and influences will have a significant impact on the inner balance of the organism. It is a finetuning exercise of the universe, whereby energies manifest in ever greater detail and complexity.

But we can't listen to all 'radio stations' at the same time, so we have to make choices. We need to decide what frequencies are appropriate to listen out for in specific circumstances and what are not. Human beings are able to either deploy antennae or withdraw them. This allows for a manageable amount of information to enter the cells, with the risk that we might 'miss something'. An individual human being decides what is important to him or her at every moment. Obviously, nature protects itself and there are certain antennae that we do not have that decision power over. You may be aware that you are not aware of making these choices either. Virtually all choices are driven by unconscious patterns we have learned in our very early development stages. It happens automatically and it is based on what you are used to, on how you have learned to function. But this means that to every individual these basic principles of life could well be different, and that is certainly the case when we look at how different cultures are focused on different aspects of life. They, as a group, make different choices what to allow in their lives and how to respond to the incoming information from nature. So, not only will there be great differences in what specific cultures find as essential elements in life, but there will also be great differences in how they respond to those elements they are taking notice of.

We make decisions to determine the way we wish to live. Obviously that doesn't necessarily need to be the same for everyone. Besides making decisions consciously, you could also say that the universe has made 'decisions' about which development path to follow. These choices are driven by energy interferences, which determine the outcome of each possibility and ultimately what creates a balance throughout the entire universe and what actually happens. That is the bigger picture, but on a more detailed scale it looks a little different.

Some antennae on the cell membranes can be either deployed or retreated. The cells belong to an individual and to the energy field of that individual. Hence, it is the state of that field that chooses which antennae to use at any given moment in time. Only information that reaches the inner workings of the cells via the antennae have an effect on the cells, and subsequently on the individual. But only those frequencies from the environment have an effect when the corresponding antenna is in use. In other words, we only connect to information in the outside world when we want to.

Obviously, these are, for the most part unconscious choices, but they are nevertheless choices the individual, or let's say the energetic being, makes. The energetic being, the energies of an individual, and the way that individual functions, the movement of those energies, is determined by its ancient background, fixed into its structure by its embryonic development, to which coping mechanisms adopted from mother were added and put into automated reaction responses. And lastly, all the knowledge gathered through his own early experiences, on which the individual now relies on in his belief of knowing the truth. All this together determines the choices of what antennae to use and when to use them. Do you want to know something? Are you interested in knowing something? The answer to such questions can be found in either heritage, mother learned coping strategies and/or selected experiences of the self. It is as if you are walking through a huge library and you only search for some books in certain sections, 'because those are the ones you are interested in'. You are, even if it is unconsciously, attracted to certain topics, to certain themes, to certain areas of the library, to certain areas of life. And anyway, you can't read or know all of the books you are presented with. In principle, your unconsciousness is connected to every book in the library. Every book in the library contains something that you have an unconscious link with, but you are choosing to read some specific books in order to increase your conscious knowledge.

This means, however, that every individual consciously only has a limited view on life. It means that there is so much more to life than one individual or one group of individuals can know consciously or even observe. One cannot see when one isn't looking. One cannot hear when one isn't listening. One cannot sense when one isn't openly and quietly receiving.

It also means that your system does not suffer from something it isn't allowing in. Your system plays a crucial role in every effect it displays, in every response it manifests. In this respect, it is true that one cannot be harmed by something one didn't know. 'Knowing' in this context is, of course, not referring to a conscious knowledge. It refers to the unconscious choice not be informed about specific aspects of the outside world. It refers to an unconscious awareness.

And this brings us to the gates of another important part of understanding life.

How do we need to understand what is meant by 'awareness' and by 'consciousness'? And how does the 'unconscious' fit into 'consciousness'?

Chapter 5

Awareness - Consciousness

Awareness is the state of knowing something. It is as simple as that. But quite how simple this is depends on what 'knowing' entails. Knowing is having extensive information or understanding. Understanding obviously is something rational; it is about intellectual faculties, about intelligence. But then again, what is considered to be 'intelligent'. You probably have heard of artificial intelligence, which indicates that there also exists another kind of intelligence. Most actual academics state that the opposite of artificial intelligence is natural intelligence. Natural Intelligence refers to the flexible ability possessed by animals, including humans, to achieve a variety of goals in different contexts, based on their rich and varied stream of experiences in the natural world. So now intelligence has nothing to do anymore with thinking and reasoning. It is the learned ability of living organisms to achieve their specific goals in life. An ability that is innate to all living creatures, from bacteria through to plants and animals. It turns out that they too 'know' a lot, but as this knowledge can't be a logical knowledge - they do not possess the capacity to think and to reason - we have to look for knowledge of a different kind in order to understand the term 'awareness' properly.

What kind of knowledge do we observe in primitive life? Well, we can see that bacteria have knowledge of what is available in their environment. They move towards a food source and away from poison. This basic knowledge is on display throughout all layers of living creatures. They are all aware of food being present in their environment and how to get to it, and they are all aware of potential danger in their environment and how to avoid it. Hence, we can state that living creatures are aware of their environment without having any intellectual knowledge. They also possess a series of preprogrammed reaction patterns that respond appropriately to the environment, once that 'awareness' is stimulated. All of this is easily explained by the antennae on the surface of every cell. These pick up frequencies, information, from the environment and they trigger, inside the cell, a preprogrammed response. So in nature, we could say that awareness of the environment is innate to all living creatures. Plain matter, as in gas, liquids and solids, does not possess such awareness. It is a specific feature of the living cell.

What is also worth noting at this point is that awareness does not require a brain or a developed nervous system. Awareness is simply an energetic connection, via frequencies, between an inner world and an outer world, separated by living matter. Hence, awareness is a feature of a living internal world that needs 'to know' what is happening outside in order to be able to maintain a balance between those two worlds.

Consciousness, however, is considered to be a brain function. Although detailed understanding of the neural mechanisms of consciousness has not been achieved, correlations between states of consciousness and functions of the brain are possible. Levels of consciousness in terms of levels of alertness or responsiveness are correlated with patterns of electrical activity of the brain. All that 'a correlation' means is that there is an indication that the two are linked. The mistake our medical scientists are making is confusing correlation with causation. Because of the link they observe, they immediately postulate that the brain effects must cause the differences seen in consciousness. They do not consider the possibility that maybe it is the changes in consciousness that create the alterations in the brain, in the neurological functioning. They also do not consider the possibility that another phenomenon, a third factor, could equally cause the brain effects as well as the consciousness effects.

When we consider the meaning of the word 'consciousness', we come across definitions like 'the state of being aware of what is around you', which is the exact definition of awareness. But equally, consciousness is defined as 'being able to think'. This is not a requirement for awareness. So it looks as if consciousness is, in essence, referring to something that has a wider spectrum than awareness. And then there is the definition of consciousness, which says 'the fact of noticing something'. And 'to notice' refers to 'paying attention, to perceive, to become aware of'. All of this guides us towards acknowledging that there now are two types of 'becoming aware'. One is being aware of what is around you, the innate natural connection an individual specimen has with its environment, and the other is a thinking awareness, linked also to paying attention. This last part of consciousness is very much related to alertness and recognition, while the first part is more linked to perception and acquaintance. We could conclude that the term 'consciousness' is used to indicate two things, whereby one is 'awareness', the part that does not involve the function of the nervous system. This is a consciousness we are not consciously aware of. The other part involves thinking and paying attention, which are consciously directed brain functions. This is a consciousness we are consciously aware of.

The unconscious mind

In psychology, the unconscious is the vast sum of operations of the mind that take place below the level of conscious awareness. The conscious mind contains all the thoughts, feelings, cognitions, and memories we acknowledge, while the unconscious consists of deeper mental processes not readily available to the conscious mind. Much learning, especially recognition of complex patterns, takes place outside of conscious awareness. Similarly, many of the elements that go into judgments and decision-making are processed outside of awareness. Intuition, too, is a product of unconscious mental operations, a set of assumptions swiftly assembled from cumulative knowledge and experience. Much of human motivation and interpersonal attraction also take shape beyond conscious awareness. Consciousness requires attention, but information can also register in the absence of directed attention. The unconscious is the repository of automatic skills, the source of stored memories, fantasy, and dreams.

The qualities of conscious thought processes are intentional, controllable, serial in nature (consumptive of limited processing resources), and accessible to awareness. No such consensus exists for the unconscious. The use of the term unconscious was originally based on one's unintentional actions and not on one's ability to process subliminal-strength information. This equation of unconscious with unintentional is how unconscious phenomena have been conceptualised and studied within social psychology for the past quarter century or so. However, social cognition research over the past 25 years has produced a stream of surprising findings regarding complex judgmental and behavioural phenomena that operate outside of awareness.

Given the uncertainty of the future and the slow rate of genetic change, our genes have provided us not with fixed responses to specific events (because these cannot be anticipated with any degree of accuracy), but with general tendencies that are adaptive across local variations (Dawkins, 1976). It is for this reason that evolution has shaped us to be open-ended systems. This openended quality gives room for 'fine-tuning' the newborn to local conditions. Much of this is given to us by human culture, the local conditions (mainly social) of the world into which we happen to be born. Dawkins (1976) noted that phenotypic plasticity enables the infant to absorb, entirely automatically, 'an already invented and largely debugged system of habits in the partly unstructured brain'. And it is not just overall cultural norms and values that are so readily absorbed during this early period of life. We also absorb the particulars of the behaviour and values of those closest to us, providing still finer tuning of appropriate-behaviour tendencies. In a review of 25 years of infant imitation research, Meltzoff (2002) concluded that young children learn much about how to behave by mere passive imitation of fellow children and also their adult caretakers. Infants in particular are wide open to such imitative tendencies, having not yet developed cognitive control structures to suppress or inhibit them. The unconscious mind collects and stores relevant information about living in the conditions the individual most likely is going to encounter.

The information comes from evolution, general human knowledge of local conditions and specific knowledge of the specific living conditions the child is going to enter into.

The open-ended nature of our evolved design has also caused us to be highly sensitive and reactive to the present and local context. Just as evolution has given us general 'good tricks' (Dennett, 1995) for survival and reproduction, and culture and early learning have fine-tuned our adaptive unconscious processes to the more specific local conditions into which we were born, contextual priming is a mechanism that provides still more precise adjustment to events and people in present time (Higgins & Bargh, 1987). In contextual priming, the mere presence of certain events and people automatically activates our representations of them, and concomitantly, all of the internal information (goals, knowledge, affect) stored in those representations that is relevant to responding back. The evolved, innate basis of these ubiquitous priming effects is revealed by the fact that they are present soon after birth, underpinning the infant's imitative abilities (see Meltzoff, 2002). Such priming effects, in which what one perceives directly influences what one does, depend on the existence of a close, automatic connection between perception and behaviour. The unconscious mind directly produces the stored picture of what we observe and experience, together with all relevant facts, and immediately, automatically, initiates a specific behaviour in response.

Evolution (as well as early learning and culture) influences our preferences and, through them, our tendencies to approach or avoid aspects of our environment. We are predisposed to prefer certain objects and aspects of our environment over others. We are often guided by our feelings, intuitions, and gut reactions, which prioritise the things that are important to do or attend to (Damasio, 1996; Schwarz & Clore, 1996). These guides do not arise out of thin air, however. Our present preferences are derived from those preferences that served adaptive ends in the past. A tenet of evolutionary theory is that evolution builds gradually on what it has to work with at that moment. Changes are slow and incremental (Allman, 2000). Knowledge gained at a lower level of blind selection

- the shortcuts and other 'good tricks' (Dennett, 1995) that consistently worked over our long-term evolutionary past - are fed upwards as a starting point and appear as a prior knowledge, the source of which we are unaware. Campbell (1974) called these 'shortcut processes' because they save us (individually) from having to figure out from scratch which processes are helpful and which are dangerous. The unconscious mind prioritises our choice in feelings, thoughts and intuitions, distilled from the pool of knowledge and information it holds, much of which is shared by a group of people that have certain background aspects of evolution in common.

The idea that action precedes reflection is not new. Several theorists have postulated that the conscious mind is not the source or origin of our behaviour. Instead, they theorise that impulses to act are unconsciously activated and that the role of consciousness is as gatekeeper and sense maker after the fact (Gazzaniga, 1985; James, 1890; Libet, 1986; Wegner, 2002). In this model, conscious processes kick in after a behavioural impulse has occurred in the brain. That is, the impulse is first generated unconsciously, and then consciousness claims (and experiences) it as its own. The unconscious mind generates the impulse for our actions, for our behaviours, which we then become consciously aware of and are able to explain and justify consciously.

All in all, the unconscious mind is the driving force behind our reaction patterns. It guides us through life. It initiates all of our behaviour and in that respect establishes a balance between the knowledge of the past and the novelty of the future. All behaviour is rooted within the old knowledge but can be adapted to new situations. When that occurs, the new experience is added to the pool of knowledge and can be used in future events. That way, we are able 'to learn new tricks'!

The conscious mind

The conscious mind is defined as the rational part of the mind that engages in deliberate thinking, reasoning, and decision-making based on sensory input, occupying less than one percent of the mind's processing power. It serves as the source of awareness, but only of a 'conscious awareness', and it requires focused attention. The conscious mind is a human attribute as it involves deliberate thinking and reasoning. Those processes are directly linked to brain activity.

When we realise that we can be aware of something without using any of our sensory organs, it makes sense that some of the mind activity occurs without using the brain and the nervous system. Our sensory organs provide information on a level we can consciously be aware of, but almost all of our awareness of life itself is an unconscious awareness. Decision making is no different. A small proportion of our decision making happens as a result of thinking and reasoning, which is a brain activity, but almost all of the decisions in life are made unconsciously. Hence, the contribution of the conscious mind to the activities in life is real but minimal. To sustain and protect life we cannot afford to hand that responsibility to a thinking mind, which only has a very small conscious pool of knowledge, a limited amount of memory data.

Episodic memory entails the capacity to encode, store, and retrieve an event, in conjunction with contextual content associated with that event. Recollecting an episode is different from recognising a past event on the basis of its familiarity. Indeed, familiarity enables us to quickly experience an event as being part of our past in the absence of memory for context. The latter is a memory function that belongs to the unconscious mind. Episodic memory is a conscious mind memory, based on a conscious recollection of a number of details specifically connected to that event. Episodic memory supports daily acts such as remembering where one has placed the keys or whether one has already taken a pill that day. Furthermore, it provides the foundation for autobiographical memory (Nelson and Fivush, 2004) and contributes to the sense of continuity of self over time. The main components of episodic memory are, in an integrated way, the 'what'/'who', 'when', and 'where' a past experience occurred. This information is gained through sensory input, which is part of the conscious mind. The stored information, this memory, serves an important purpose in human life, but is not essential to its survival. The information required for survival is stored in the unconscious mind.

Conclusions

- Awareness has two components: a very large unconscious awareness and a very small conscious awareness
- The unconscious knows everything about life
- The unconscious regulates life, plans life, protects life, steers life and powers life
- The conscious allows us to observe life, including our own actions, thoughts and feelings
- The conscious allows us to gradually become more consciously aware of the structure of life and of the function of the unconscious
- The conscious learns to become more aware of life, including itself

The conscious mind is connected to logic. The unconscious mind is connected to reality, and reality is a product of evolution. The 'meaning' of reality is built in to the unconscious mind and does not require a 'logic' explanation. However, the conscious mind is constantly looking for a 'logical' meaning to life. In order for life *to make sense*, to the conscious mind, it needs to find logic in the reality it is faced with. Hence, every individual conscious mind is either finding 'meaning' of not finding meaning in the events, depending on whether or not it is capable of finding some sort of logic. When it is able to piece a particular picture together, using some of the pieces it is conscious of, the conscious mind will give meaning to life, while in fact, nothing happens without meaning, a fact that is already recognised by the unconscious mind.

When looking to understand life or to explain what is happening in life, you can only find those answers in the unconsciousness. Although the conscious mind is making decisions in life based on consciously gathered knowledge and on rational thinking, it can never provide true answers to origins and reasons for habits, deeds, thoughts, beliefs and feelings. The truth behind all of these is to be found in energetic interference patterns, not in logic.

Once again, life is not logical. So what makes you think that to explain something in life you need logic?

Chapter 6

Our Reality

There are two contributing systems to the creation of our reality: the conscious and the unconscious mind. Both are entry gates through which an energetic spark is being picked up as a signal that requires a response. Both systems are triggered by energetic interferences that alert the inner world of the individual. The initial effect is the creation of a sensation or of a feeling, caused by the energy shift in the outside world of the individual. A sensation is different from a perception, which is clearly information entering the system via perceptive organs. The process of sensing is non-physical. One can sense being watched. One can sense danger, before being actually exposed to it. One can sense things before we perceive them. Once we become aware of a sensation, it triggers questions. Now the brain gets involved, which is part of the conscious mind, and it wants to know 'what am I feeling?', 'why am I feeling it?' and 'where does the feeling come from?'. We start to think about it. Once we have figured out what it is all about, we decide on a plan of action. Our brain decides on a plan of action. At least that is what human society is teaching us. We are learning to weigh up the risks. We are learning to anticipate the danger. We are learning to be sensible about life. When we force our actions to be 'sensible', to be a conscious reaction, we are trying to override what the system would do naturally and how it would respond naturally, in balance with the internal field of the individual.

However, that same energetic spark has been picked up by an antenna on the cell membrane, which sets off a preprogrammed response within the cells of the body. It is a coordinated response of all cells to a change in the field that surrounds the individual. This happens automatically and very fast. It doesn't involve asking questions and 'figuring out' the answers. Hence, life has an immediate answer ready, which will ensure the balance between inner world and outer world is maintained. And then the conscious mind comes up with an answer! Now it wants to have its say in the matter.

If we are not quick to implement what the conscious mind proposes to do but instead we allow a little time to pass, we can already observe the effect of the adjustment the unconscious mind has executed. If we now allow the conscious mind to take note of this effect and include it in our logical approach to the situation, it turns out that every time we could simply continue the action the system has already started on the instruction of the unconscious mind. We may find ourself consciously doing nothing at all and quietly waiting. We may find ourself already in the midst of an action that we gratefully follow through, such as raising an arm to deflect the incoming projectile. So the main danger is twofold here. One is that we consciously act too quickly, before taking into account the information of the effect of the already implemented unconscious response. And the other one is that we consciously implement a response that is different from the unconscious response. Why are these reactions dangerous? Because the unconscious mind has already implemented the most appropriate of responses, so believing we can consciously improve on that is dangerous in terms of maintaining the internal balance of our being. As it can't be improved upon, the conscious response must be of a lower quality, must be less appropriate, less accurate.

It pays you to be patient, to wait, not to hurry. It pays you to observe rather than to do. It pays you to look out for intuition rather than for logic. Human society is built on logic, nature is built on energies, and the layer that has the closest contact with the energy field itself, is expressed in a sensation, a feeling. So, when dealing with parts of life that has its roots in human society, is organised by human society and is governed by human society, you would do well to approach it with a logical mind. If you are able to identify the logical pathways of the construction, you can navigate the danger zones quite easily and you will find solutions to all problems. However, when dealing with nature, with life issues, which is organised by energies and is governed by the laws of energy interactions, you would do well to ignore logic and to follow the direction of what you feel. Follow your gut feeling, go where your heart wants to take you. It may seem weird to you that we are simultaneously living in two completely different worlds.

But that isn't really the case. It appears that way, but the reality is quite different. There only exists one kind of life. Life is one format in which the creation process is expressing itself. Life is part of the creation. Within that process, human life appears and that is part of the same creation process, adhering to the same creation laws. Hence, human life is, in essence, no different from any other life and it follows the same rules as all the other lifeforms. There is no escaping this. However, humans are trying to do just that. They are trying to create a life that is the opposite to what it really is. Make it into a logical structure so everything becomes predictable to the humans who have created this illusion of a logical life. Build a structure you understand and control, and force everyone to fit into it, which gives you control over what happens within that structure, within life itself. Just as nature controls all of life because it created it, humans are trying to create a kind of life they can control. In the first phase, a group of people will endeavour to create a human life that binds humans together under their control, but as a separate unit within the natural life of humans. In a later phase, they will try and move the separate life of controlled humans out of the existing natural life of nature. In opposition to the natural life, they will call it a virtual life or an artificial life, which creates a virtual reality based on artificial intelligence.

The reality humans are living in is twofold, but one part is locked into the other. There are two pathways into the creation of our reality. The reality of our lives is the result of the choices we make and the actions we take, and that can be achieved in two separate ways. On the one hand, we have the natural pathway of life whereby the unconscious connection we have with the rest of creation, and consequently with our environment, provides us with the stimuli that will take life in a specific direction, always in harmony with itself and its surroundings. It creates our reality through the instigation of feelings and thoughts. On the other hand, we have the conscious human mind that uses logic to elicit emotions, which in turn manufactures thoughts, leading us to take action. It creates actual actions through bringing about emotions based on rational thinking. Careful observation allows us to differentiate between the two systems. In the natural way of creation, the feelings arise first, and when we are able to 'catch' it at an early stage, we have to admit we don't actually know why we are feeling this way. Then, when we start to think about it, we come up with a logical line that justifies the feeling. The thought follows the feeling, which leads to our action. In the human introduction of reality, using the conscious mind pathway, we first make a judgement on what we observe through our senses, which in turn stirs up emotions, which leads to our action.

With regards to your inner balance, it is extremely important to recognise which pathway you are using in your life, as the only manner in which you are able to maintain harmony in yourself and with your environment is to follow the natural path of creation. Remaining connected to nature and the natural processes guides us on the road of least resistance towards our personal destination. And that, by the way, is not to live the longest possible life, but to live the most harmonious of lives. Your personal destination is set by the nature of your life, not by another human deciding for you what would be the best course of action for you.

Life how it has been structured to function

Allow me to illustrate how life could work well for everybody, given the way it is created and the way it functions. Hear me out. Let it sink in. Allow a feeling to emerge from within. See if what your conscious mind comes up with matches your inner sense of reality.

My life is like a house. It has separate rooms for different activities, equipped to facilitate those specific activities in those specific places. It has windows that allow me to look in certain directions, looking at the things that are important to me to observe in the world around me. The front door is always closed but never locked. Nobody will enter my space uninvited. My house is where I am the boss. I can do what I want, when I want and where I want. There is nobody to criticise me or correct me. It is a place where I am safe, secure and able to totally be myself. It is where I can find peace, where I can be most creative, where I can be free from outside dangers.

My house stands alone in a street where there are other houses. The street is part of a larger area of houses, an estate, which is a part of a village, a collection of houses. The village lies within a nation, that is part of a continent on earth. My life is part of other people's lives, friends and family (living in my street), which is a part of all my acquaintances (living in the village). Together with others, we are part of a regional group of people, sharing common treats. This forms part of a culture of people, which is a section of a human race on earth.

From the moment I step outside of my house, I enter a world that is not entirely mine anymore. Lots more people are using that space. So I need to be aware of others during my time in that communal space. When I want to sit down, I need to ask whether the seat has been taken, even though nobody is sitting on it right now. The seat might be occupied by the person just having vacated it for a short period of time with the intention of definitely returning to it soon enough. Or the seat might be used by someone everyday at five o'clock and it is now five to five. Of course, I can just take the seat as I observe it to be vacant right at this moment, but by doing so I am creating conflict. Not taking into account the needs of others whilst being present in a shared space will simply stir up trouble. At the same time, the others will have to take note of my personal needs too. If, for instance, I need to sit down because I have just broken my ankle, my personal requirements are, at that moment, much higher than the reason given why the seat is already 'reserved'. Important in this concept, whilst bearing in mind that nobody wants to create conflict, is that the evaluation of my own needs compared to the needs of others is done by others, not by myself. To me, my needs are always more important than the needs of others because I am the one experiencing the difficulty, the inconvenience and the panic.

I have to be mindful not to enter someone else's personal space. Nobody is allowed to enter my house, my personal space, so I am not allowed to enter someone else's either. When it does happen, and it will, I immediately apologise and leave when the person points out to me where I am and what I am doing. When I am invited into someone's space, I take note of the rules of engagement of the host. I behave in a manner the host requests. If I do not feel like doing that or at some point I feel I cannot comply, I apologise and I leave.

Entering someone's house, personal space, is more of a mental interference than an actual physical occurrence. Life is a field of interacting energies, which is also how humans meet and interact, on a non-physical plane long before they interact on a physical level.

As I do not want anybody to tell me how I should live my life and how I should behave in my own space, I myself also do not have the right to tell others what to do. The house is a safe place where I can be myself, no matter how I feel or who I am. Any interference from the outside world into my home, into my personal space, threatens my essential existence. Moving into the communal space I have to take note of the others as they have to take note of me. What happens in the communal space when someone imposes set rules for human interactions and human behaviour?

Occupying the communal space by enforcing certain specific behaviour immediately excludes other behaviour. It discriminates against all other possible ways of 'being'. Within the natural communal space free interactions happen and they are judged and controlled by the people doing the interacting. When I want to sit down, whether or not I can use that seat depends on the person I am asking, not on a rule that says I have to be of a certain height to be allowed to make use of that particular seat. When the decision is made on the spot by the people directly involved in the exchange, then the decision is completely depended upon the moment itself, involving all the circumstances of that moment. Hence, one moment the answer may be that I can use the seat, and another time I can't. If it turns out my needs outweigh the needs of others in that moment, different decisions from the expected one can be made by the people directly involved in the exchange. No set rules, not for everybody, not for all the times and not for all circumstances, should exist if the community is to support the needs of the individual. And no individual should rigidly hold on to his own rules of engagement without allowing space for the requirements of the moment.

Harmony can only be achieved when there is flexibility in the moment. Electromagnetic interactions are momentarily active, all depending on the conditions of the moment. There is no general ruling that forces a specific event to happen in a specific preset way, when the circumstances are not ideal for it.

In my own space I am free to feel, think and judge. In my own space I only have to adhere to my own rules and I make those up as I go along. Outside of my own space, I need to consider other people's feelings, thoughts and judgements and I need to consider their reaction to the expression of my own personal stuff. When I know my opinion is causing others distress or pain or confusion then I do not express my personal views in that way in the communal space to those people. And others do the same in respect to me. I share my personal views with people who ask, not with people who are disturbed by it.

Having a feeling or a thought about something is completely different from acting upon it. I am free, in my own space, within myself, to have any feeling or thought I want to have and to change it whenever I see fit. I do not have that same freedom to act upon it, because that triggers a variety of interactions in the communal space. Hence, it disturbs the harmony within the communal space. I can decide not to allow certain people or information to enter my private space. I cannot demand that those people stay out of the street my house stands in or that people spread that information outside my window. So I am aware of the controversy of some of my feelings and thoughts within the communal space and so I am careful not to cause conflict there. On the other hand, when one is confronted by disturbing feelings and thoughts, one retreats from the conflict back into one's own safe space. The community will become aware of my reaction and take note not to evoke that same disturbed feeling within me. Taking note of the effect one has caused allows one to adjust one's behaviour in future interactions. When everybody does this, conflicts will be acute events and won't be repeated.

Each house is a space governed by the owner and by nobody or nothing else. Outside the houses, where there are interactions between individuals, there needs to be attention given to the environment one engages in. That environment is governed by the people who are present at that time and by nobody or nothing else.

Conflict is avoided by paying attention to the needs of others within the communal space. When a conflict arises then the opposing parties both recognise their own contribution towards the electromagnetic potential they together have created, and both parties retreat to allow the built-up energy to subside.

Then we all live in a house that is called Harmony, in a street called Harmony, on an estate called Harmony, in a village called Harmony, part of a nation called Harmony on a continent called Harmony, somewhere on earth.

But what happens when two people want to share their lives? The same rules apply here. Each need to preserve an inner space that they own, a space where they can have their own feelings, thoughts and create their own actions. They need to have the freedom not to have to consider anybody or anything else. But they also want to share, want to join their lives together, which means they want to share, to join, their actions, thoughts and feelings. So they create a communal sphere between them. Within that sphere, one has to consider the needs of the other and together they then decide which priority to go for. When ideas and feelings do not conform, a decision has to be made which one to choose, which direction to follow. Hence, one direction is preferred over the other. How can this be done without creating a conflict?

Priority is where one thing is more important than another thing. How do we evaluate the importance, so both individuals can agree? The importance is evaluated by the effect the choice will have on the internal balance of each person involved. The more it will disturb the inner harmony, the more weight it adds to not choose that option. The more it supports the inner harmony, the greater the inclination to choose this option. The more important issue here is the potential disturbance, which takes priority over the potential support of the harmony. Together they choose not to do what seriously disrupts the inner harmony of one. Hence, the other person recognises this very important issue and agrees to avoid the considered action.

And then there is the chosen exception! Another aspect of our reality is that remaining within our comfort zone is not going to allow us to evolve much. The comfort zone is where we try to maintain the same balance all the time, but there are times when it is time to move on. This is done by disturbing the existing balance in order to move towards a new one. This is more easily done when there is someone with you to support you during this process, during this scary, uncertain, transition. Hence, together the decision can be made not to choose to support the existing balance but to move on into new territory for one of you. Bear in mind that this should always have the full support of the individual whose balance is being disturbed. The other person's obligation is to be aware of this process and to allow it to move through the various adjustment stages. Always take your cues from the person within the process. Never try and force someone else's transition process.

Our reality is a continual learning process to adapt both the inner space and the communal space to the constantly changing influences. The individual learns from his own position and encounters, and the group learns from the encounters with the various individuals. Our reality is constantly changing but it does so following the same pathway, adhering to the same interaction laws. Our reality is to learn these laws, to come to know what our true reality Is.

Chapter 7

Dreaming

'A dream is a succession of images, dynamic scenes and situations, ideas, emotions, and sensations that usually occur involuntarily in the mind during certain stages of sleep.' Dreaming is not caused by complex brain activity. Complex brain activity is the physical manifestation of dreaming, not the other way around.

Dreaming occurs 'involuntarily', which already proves it isn't a brain activity, as the brain is about the conscious mind and therefore whatever activity is generated by the brain has, at some level, a logic to it. Dreaming is, however, a spontaneous involuntary occurrence 'in the mind', to be more precise, in the unconscious mind. The unconscious mind – we are asleep and unaware! – produces images, ideas, emotions and sensations. The manifestation of a dream follows the same creation pattern as all other forms of creation. It begins with a sensation. This becomes more 'real', more physical, when it is being expressed in the form of images. These are a representation of the sensation that whirls around in the unconscious mind. These images, when they become even more realistic, expressed in a more condensed format, become ideas. Why do I get the 'best' ideas when I am asleep? Because they arise straight from our unconsciousness, which is the real 'me. It is the direct connection to who I truly am and so any idea that has its roots in the unconsciousness has been formed by the real me and therefore truly benefits me.

The unconscious mind is constantly active. This movement is the source of our life. Without the constant movement of energies within the unconscious mind there would be no life. The unconscious mind is constantly adjusting to the moving energies of its surroundings, from our direct living conditions to the universe itself. This activity is not interrupted by us being awake. Our conscious mind only provides another highway of information reaching the unconscious, where constant adjustments are happening to maintain a balance and to ensure that the entity is kept together, alive and 'well'. When we are awake, all our conscious space is taken up by our alertness, directed to the outside world. We are unaware of any inner movement, or even of the existence of our unconscious mind. This changes when we fall asleep.

By switching off our consciousness we drastically reduce the information influx from our direct environment to our inner self, to our unconscious mind, to our 'self' energies. During sleep, the mind is no longer burdened by our daily worries, fears, hopes and expectations. It no longer has to deal with any of that and it has the opportunity to turn its attention inwardly. Now all its energy can be concentrated on what is really happening at the core of your being. Now it can busy itself balancing the inner energies with the aim to keep it all functioning as smoothly as possible, without you consciously interfering, telling it what is important, what is true and what you want. Now it is all about your real priorities, your real truth and your real needs. This is all about how to keep you alive and functioning well.

The reality of the disturbance of the inner energetic field of the individual creates sensations during deep sleep. Energies are moved. Energies are interacting with each other and they become more balanced. Larger disturbances create sensations, which may become images. Some of these images we become aware of.

Most of our dreams remain hidden in our unconsciousness. However, the greater the disturbance becomes within the deeper layers of the unconscious, the more ripples will appear on the surface of the mind, which is the conscious mind. The conscious mind may become aware of some of the activity within the unconscious mind, when this activity is vicious enough to ripple through large sections of the unconscious. While we remain in a deep sleep, we cannot become conscious of our dreams. There are only two ways in which this awareness can happen.

One is that the disturbance of the energetic waves in the mind is of such an order that it 'shakes' the existing balance within the conscious mind, on the surface of the mind, the layers on top of the unconscious mind. We wake up suddenly, with a flash of a certain reality going through our conscious mind. What was that? We are aware of a specific 'situation' we found ourselves in. It was a weird scene. Doesn't make any sense. But it felt real. In fact, it was real. It was real in the sense that your unconscious mind did create this image from a real sensation that originated within the deeper layers of your unconscious mind. Hence, it is very real to you. In fact, it is more real to you than much of the human world you consciously move around in. The image is only a representation of what is going on inside your energetic field and the tensions that have arisen there. However, the sensation that produced this image is very real. Try to identify and to hold on to the sensation. Let go of the image and of trying to interpret the image. You are entering a field of manipulation and misdirection by 'experts'. All that matters, all that is truly real, is the sensation you feel. Do you feel fear? Do you feel anger? Do you feel frustration? Do you feel ignored?

Isn't it striking that when you suddenly wake up, popping out of a dream, you never feel elated. There is never an overwhelming feeling of joy and happiness. The driving force that wakes you is always what we call 'negative' feelings. These are not really negative; they are feelings of warning. These are literally 'wakeup' calls. Your unconscious mind is screaming at you to become alert to very disturbing energies in your life. It wants to get the message across to make changes to your relationship with your environment, to how you stand in life, because what is entering your system requires so much energy to rebalance the system that, in the long term, it won't be sustainable. You urgently need to deal with the sensation your unconscious mind is alerting you to. If you are being woken up by a dream, take note of the sensation, because this is what your inner self is struggling with. Fear means that something in your daily life is threatening your existence. Play detective and go and find out what it is, so you can make conscious decisions about it. Whatever the sensation is you feel at the moment of waking, investigate what creates that same feeling in your everyday environment and change it. That is if you are truly looking for a mindful peaceful life.

The second way we can become consciously aware of a dream is during a dozing phase. We are still asleep but only just underneath the conscious surface. We are just becoming slightly aware of some of our surroundings without feeling the need to actively engage in it. In that state, we may also get images that move into our consciousness from the deeper levels, from the unconscious, because the conscious mind is not that active as to suppress all that comes from the inside. However, these images can only come from the upper regions of the unconscious. Our consciousness does not have direct access to the deep layers of the unconscious. We are not allowed to take a direct look at the inner workings of life itself. Given the arrogant way the conscious mind of the human being is behaving, forcing human life in a direction opposite to its natural path, it is a lifesaving restriction we can be forever grateful for.

In this semi-sleep state, we can become aware of images that have been created in the unconscious. These never have the same forceful impact than the ones that wake you suddenly out of a deep sleep. These are more gentle in nature. However, they do represent a sensation, a message, from your inner self, from your unconsciousness. Hence, it would be wise to take note. This is where 'the good idea' arises from. Because it originates from within, not from your brain activity, not from your restricted logical thinking. This is the real you giving you a hint, not a jolt, about what to do next.

Dream analysis is in fact dream interpretation. Interpretation is different from meaning. While meaning is defined as 'the inherent significance or definition of a word, phrase, text, or symbol, which is said to be objective', interpretation is subjective, as in 'interpretation involves the process of explaining or making sense of something, often based on personal or contextual factors'. Hence, the 'meaning' of a dream can never be known, as we do not know how the unconscious mind defines the images it produces. So all that is left is interpretation, which is a way of giving personal meaning to the images. Here you have a choice, either you accept the personal interpretation of an expert or you stick to your own personal interpretation. What does it mean to you? It is futile to be looking for the 'real' meaning of a dream. It is what it feels like to you. Don't waste any time and energy on figuring out what the dream means, when it is much more valuable to accept what it feels like to you. It is your dream, images that come forth from sensations that have sprung from interactions of your own energies. Concentrate on what feeling the dream evokes and not on the images. Learn to 'feel' the interpretation, rather than rationally analyse the dream in terms of meaning given to symbols, context and words.

And then there is the phenomenon of daydreaming. Daydreaming is a stream of consciousness that detaches from current external tasks when one's attention becomes focused on a more personal and internal direction. While you are awake, your conscious mind wonders of, away from its focus on the outer world, turning more inwardly. There are many types of daydreams. However, the most common characteristic to all forms of daydreaming meets the criteria for mild dissociation. The medical profession is quick to make the process of dissociation into a disorder, while in fact it can be beneficial for creativity, problem-solving, and future planning. Maybe that is exactly why the medical profession sees it as a disorder!

In circumstances of a quiet conscious mind, where there isn't much disturbance, where not much potential danger exists that requires our constant attention and alertness, the conscious mind has an opportunity 'to talk to' the unconscious mind. Even though they are inherently connected to one another, the conscious mind does not have much 'spare' time in our modern society to take clues from the unconscious mind. Too busy! During quiet moments, however, it may just sink to the lower levels of consciousness, closer to the upper levels of unconsciousness. Here it is able to pick up some ripples, some energy flow, that never reaches the surface of consciousness when that is being bombarded by information streaming in from the outside world. Keep the minds of the people busy so they do not create ideas by themselves!

If you really want to solve the problems your life is being confronted with then you would do well to quiet the conscious mind and to become aware, within that stillness, of what your inner self really needs you to do. All the messages you need are there, but if you never listen, it will appear to you as if life is a complete mystery. If you do have the feeling that life is a mystery, that everything is left to chance, that nothing in life makes sense, then you are not consciously connected to your unconscious self. Time to start dreaming, and you may want to start this process while you are awake.

Chapter 8

Behaviour

Understanding human behaviour involves understanding how life is structured and how it operates. Behaviour is nothing more than the way an organism acts. It refers to observable actions conducted by the organism. To understand what is happening, to understand these actions, we need to know how life is structured and functions.

The physical expression of life is constructed on a three layer basis. Life itself is a physical manifestation of an energy spectrum into a cell form. Now there is energy flowing inside this form as well as outside and there is a constant back and forth action-reaction pattern that ensures the inside world of the organism stays in touch, stays in balance, with its surroundings. As the lifeform becomes more and more complex the three layers of functioning are revealed. It all starts with a stimulus that has its origin in a differential in electromagnetic potential between inside and outside of the life structure and in differences of pressures on part of the system. This trigger creates at first a change in internal flow. It can be noticed as a sensation, a feeling. This sensation in turn manifests in a more concrete form, which we can recognise as thoughts that express the essence of this feeling. These thoughts then lead to an action, which is seen as behaviour.

The pathway of physical manifestation is always the same. Increased pressure compresses the energies, making them more concrete, more fixed in smaller but more readily identifiable 'bits'. Hence, in higher evolved animal species, behaviour, actions, follow thought, which is an expression of a feeling, a sensation. What sparks this process is an energetic push, a stimulus, an energetic flow in reaction to an energetic change in the field. We already know that life is being directed by the unconscious mind, which means that our behaviour is an expression of fluctuations within the unconscious mind. The feelings we may be consciously aware of, as well as the thoughts we may be consciously aware of, are underlying our actions and are in tune with the underlying unconscious mind as well as with the overlying physical behaviour. Some of our behaviour, our actions, are supported by the conscious awareness of the way it manifests. Sometimes we are aware of what we feel and what we think. This is the reason why an individual is able to justify his actions. Even murder is, at that time, in that moment, perfectly justifiable to the perpetrator.

But behaviour only requires the unconscious mind. It has no desire for a conscious awareness. Everything functions perfectly well without it. *Blessed are the poor in spirit*. Conscious awareness only plays a part in being able to follow the unconscious pathway from sensation through to action.

The mind

In order for life to function, only the unconscious mind is required. It sparks life. It gives it direction. It supports it. And yet, at the very latest stages of animal development we see the emergence of a conscious mind, a mind that has a conscious awareness of its surroundings and of the self as a separate entity within the energy bubble of life.

Consciousness is, as we have stated, linked to rationality, to thinking. It is a brain function. It develops under impulse of the development of the physical senses. It uses input from the sensory organs to create pictures and structures that make sense. In evolutionary terms, this is a development that appears very late on the time scale, which once more proves that a conscious mind is not necessary to sustain life itself. This begs the question: "what is it good for?" Or "what purpose does it serve?"

Life is an expression of energetic interactions, creating, in the first instance, sensations within the inner field of the organism. The organism simply senses what to do. Its entire behavioural pattern is governed by the unconscious awareness of its environment. As lifeforms become more complex a conscious awareness becomes more obvious, even though life still continues being driven by the unconscious mind.

The senses pick up information from the environment, from the outside world, that we are aware of, unlike our cells, which continue to pick up information from the environment that we are not aware of. Hence, the latter is information that feeds the unconscious mind, while the sensory organs feed information to the conscious mind. It may be obvious to you that the sensory organs have a very limited range from which they can pick up information, compared to the range that the set of antennae on the cell membrane cover. However, we now do have a conscious awareness of our surroundings, albeit a very limited one.

When this information enters the living system, it is being processed in much the same way as the information entering the cell. In the first place it creates a sensation, a feeling. When we see something, when we hear something, it 'grabs' us, it fills us with a specific sense. The difference now is that we become consciously aware of this sensation, which filters through in thought terms. The feeling becomes a thought, which we sometimes allow to manifest itself into words, into an ordered form of sentences and speech. And sometimes we feel the need to act upon this sensation and these corresponding thoughts. So the conscious mind, just as the unconscious mind, produces feelings, thoughts and actions. The three step process in the unconscious mind is mostly hidden out of sight, out of reach for our conscious mind, while the same three step process from sensory information is much more accessible to our conscious awareness. Here we can follow 'the logic' of the steps in someone else's life, even if we don't agree with it.

Observing and judging another person's actions, behaviour, is a rational process, which makes it very useful if we are trying to understand behaviour that is being directed by the conscious mind of that person. When there is a 'logical' explanation for the behaviour, we can all follow the reasoning behind it, although we may prefer to make different choices ourselves. What is clear, however, is the fact that we are able to follow someone else's logical line from feelings to thought to actions. This is important because we like to know. This statement ignores the fact that the unconscious mind already knows! But that is not good enough to us. We want the brain, our conscious awareness, to know.

So the conscious mind is gradually becoming knowledgeable about what the unconscious mind already knows. The conscious mind is learning from the unconscious mind. The unconscious mind is the teacher and the conscious mind is the pupil. The unconscious mind is the seat of knowledge, while the conscious mind is the void of ignorance. The unconscious mind is the parent and the conscious mind is the child. Luckily the unconscious mind is providing us with guidance in life.

Or, at least, it has done so far.

But there is a problem. If a stimulus, either coming in via the unconscious mind or via the conscious mind, produces a feeling, which evolves into thoughts, which become an action, then how are we able to distinguish the source? Is this even relevant? Oh yes, it is, as the unconscious mind is the real guidance in life, is holding the knowledge of life, and the creations of the conscious mind are fantasy constructions, a random configuration of single pieces of information One we most certainly must rely on and the other we most certain should not.

It is impossible to make this distinction using your conscious mind, because the conscious mind is unable to see beyond the manifestation itself, beyond the thought or feeling. But if we remain alert and aware of the two possibilities, rather than believing one must be the correct one to follow because it is logical, the answer will be shown to us. As nature, life, is all about keeping a balance within an ever changing field, every change in the field will get a response. So instead of worrying about whether we have made the right choice or not, whether a certain action is the right one for us to do, we could simply do it and watch for the response. If what happens next is obstructing where we consciously think we need to go, then the universe, the energies of life, by causing friction, tell us not to do it. When everything runs smoothly and 'it all falls into place', the message is to carry on.

One consideration to this system of judgement of information. In order to be 100% sure about the answer, it sometimes is useful to either repeat the action or to put more effort into it. If we really would like to try a specific road in our life, we do need to be adamant about it. Don't force or manipulate it, but be firm, put a lot of effort into it, and try again (sometimes it is the right thing to do but at the wrong time or the wrong place). The universe will give you the truthful answer to the question you are asking.

Behaviour

Human behaviour is driven by the unconscious mind, which provides in survival needs of nourishment, safety and procreation. Because it has information on all levels of natural functioning, it is able to guide us to a balance that can be adjusted to each and every change in the outer as well as the inner world (ageing process). It creates actions, following the pathway of creation, out of feelings that become thoughts that become actions. One doesn't have to think about it. One doesn't have to explain anything. One simply has to follow one's instincts.

But since the conscious mind came into existence, life has become a little more complicated. The conscious mind gathers its own information via its own channels. These channels, the sensory organs, are directing their 'antennae' onto the physical manifestation of creation. It scans, in its limited range, the physical outer world for clues and information. It collects this information and it starts to puzzle with it. It tries to create 'a picture that makes sense', out of the few pieces it was able to gather. The information that reaches the inner world via the conscious mind is far more restricted than the range of energies the unconscious mind has access to. And yet, the conscious mind busies itself 'to understand' the world, 'to understand' life.

Just like a child is trying to understand the adult world, the conscious mind is trying to make sense of the living world, of nature. Just like a child is connecting pieces of information and coming up with explanations for what it feels, thinks and does, so is the conscious mind looking for reasonable explanations of human experiences. And just like a child fails to understand adult life completely, the conscious mind fails to understand life, nature and even itself. But, just as the child thinks it knows it all, the conscious mind is arrogant enough to claim knowledge and wisdom.

It doesn't sound like a good idea to allow a child to make the fundamental decisions in life for the entire family. That should still be an adult job. That is, if you are still able to recognise the fact that a child, no matter how smart it is, has too little experience of life and is therefore not the best person to make decisions about life. Well, the same reasoning should stand with regards to the conscious mind. It simply doesn't have enough knowledge of life, of nature, to be allowed to dictate the direction human life should take. Just as responsible parents should stand up to guide their child, to deny it certain wishes and desires, so should we allow the unconscious mind, our intuition, to be our guide in life, to deny us our certain wishes and desires. Not what the conscious mind wants in life is what is important, but what the unconscious mind actually produces, actually manifests, is what is important.

Within a family, the structure favours the parents as being 'the boss' because the power that keeps the family together and powers the family as a unit lies in the hands of the parents. They are the ones who provide the essential requirements in life to the child, such as nourishment and safety. This gives them more cloud to implement their will. However, once you start to undermine the power of the parents within the family structure, you hand power to the children, the seat of ignorance, the encyclopedia that still needs to be written. In nature, in life, all the consciousness is in the hands of the ignorant conscious mind and when that one declares that it knows everything and is ready to take over intelligence, then the counterweight, the messages from the unconsciousness, is only provided in silence, in expressions that can only be noticed when one pays attention. And that is not something the power crazy child is willing to consider.

Now, human behaviour is on the one hand natural, rooted in the way nature operates, in the way it has always done it and will always continue to do it, and on the other hand human, emerging from the darkness of ignorance. Both systems create a reality through instigating feelings, turning into thoughts, which are being organised in a logical fashion, leading to behaviour. The part of human behaviour that is based on the logic of how pieces of information are being put together can easily be recognised in the fact that it changes continuously. As the conscious mind gathers a new piece of information it changes the picture it painted of reality. As the information changes, we are then told to organise that information differently, which results in a different picture of life and consequently in a different direction humanity is steered into. The climate on earth has always fluctuated between very hot and very cold. It has always gone up and down the scale of the available spectrum. That is what nature is about, moving from one end of the scale and back again, and each time the universe 'learns' something different from the journey. That is the natural way, the unconscious way. When humanity, the conscious way, decides that fluctuations in climate are only due to the CO_2 in the atmosphere, we create an entire story on such a premise. The picture we, consciously, put together is limited by the information we care to take into account.

The impact of the interference on life in general increases dramatically when humanity prefers explanations they compile within the conscious mind. In principle, when the conscious mind is here to learn from the unconscious mind, then it is no disaster that the conscious mind disagrees with the unconscious mind and tries to do it differently. Children don't, and neither should they, agree with what their parents are doing, believing or enforcing. However, allowing each individual to find out in his own conscious mind what is true and what isn't, is how humanity as a whole is going to progress towards truth and knowledge, but when the ideas of a few are being implemented in the lives of others, when a few children in the class are deciding that no child should read certain books or study certain subjects, the level of real intelligence, the amount of knowledge held by the population of children, will reduce dramatically. And human behaviour will dramatically change as a result. Following the conscious mind on issues of life and nature, being logical about it, is disastrous to the development of human beings.

Behavioural disorders

In the first place it is good to know that the medical profession, blessed with the power of diagnosing illnesses and disorders, does not provide us with a definition of 'normal behaviour'. I wonder how one decides what is abnormal, a disorder, in the absence of a clear idea of what is normal. Well, if a behaviour of any person is such that it is socially and culturally not acceptable and is creating nuisance in the personal and social sphere, it is considered as a Behavioural Disorder. Socially and culturally unacceptable behaviour. So the behaviour can be perfectly natural, but if a specific society or culture doesn't approve of it, it is deemed a disorder, an illness. And who is in charge of society then? Who decides what to include in a culture and what not? It's governments who make laws and rules on behalf of the people. Governments represent the people of the country, of the society. They are elected by the people of the country, of the society, but they are presented to the people, as candidates who are willing to represent them, by groups and organisations that have a tremendous interest in *how* society is governed. In short, big industry, the drivers of the economy of the society, will have their representatives in government, and because the economy is seen as the most important factor within society – not the wellbeing of the citizen! – it is their voice that is considered the most important. In real terms, no government can remain in power when it doesn't follow the wishes of the economy, of the industry. One of the main contributors to the economy is the medical industry, which also happens to be the industry that has the power to diagnose disorders. And they can decide that something must be classified as a disorder, even if they fail to identify what is normal. Behavioural Disorders are medical illness conditions when they, the representatives and protectors of society, determine this to be the case.

The medical profession is happy to state: "No one knows the actual cause or causes of emotional disturbance, although several factors — heredity, brain disorder, diet, stress, and family functioning — have been suggested and vigorously researched. A great deal of research goes on every day, but to date, researchers have not found that any of these factors are the direct cause of behavioural or emotional problems." Are you getting this? The medical profession decides that certain behaviour is a disorder, because it is socially or culturally unacceptable, while they do admit that they don't know any cause for this disorder. Could it just be possible that the kind of behaviour they are referring to forms part of the normal spectrum of human behaviour, but that the problem really is that they don't like it? In which case it helps a lot if you are the boss and you have the power to decide that something is unacceptable. No known cause, but they are going to treat these disorders as it is definitely something that needs to be dealt with.

Let's follow the medical profession on their journey through their descriptions of behavioural disorders.

• Attention Deficit/Hyperactivity Disorder (ADHD) - This is defined as a developmental disorder marked by persistent symptoms of inattention and/or hyperactivity and impulsivity that interfere with functioning or development.

• Obsessive-Compulsive Disorder (OCD) - This is a long-lasting disorder in which a person experiences uncontrollable and recurring thoughts (obsessions), engages in repetitive behaviours (compulsions), or both.

• Autism Spectrum Disorder (ASD) - This is a neurological and developmental disorder that affects how people interact with others, communicate, learn, and behave. Autism is known as a 'spectrum' disorder because there is wide variation in the type and severity of symptoms people experience.

* Bipolar Disorder - Bipolar disorder (formerly called manic-depressive illness or manic depression) is a mental illness that causes unusual shifts in a person's mood, energy, activity levels, and concentration. Unlike simple mood swings, each extreme episode of bipolar disorder can last for several weeks (or even longer). These shifts can make it difficult to carry out day-to-day tasks.

Nicely put! However, whatever the behaviour is, whatever actions an individual takes, it is the end phase of a three step process. An energetic stimulus creates a sensation, which in turn creates thoughts, which result in an action. Whether or not these actions fit into a set pattern of 'acceptable' behaviour is a different matter altogether. If there is something wrong within this sequence of how actions come about then one should seriously consider it to be abnormal, and seek intervention. If however the problem is that the action does not fit into an artificially created (not natural) framework of what is acceptable or not, then one might want to intervene too, in which case the focus should be on the inappropriate framework and not on the feeling/thought/action, which in itself is not 'wrong'. If I desperately need to go to the toilet and there is no toilet facility anywhere near, then my action is one that is named 'wild toileting'. This is an offence. It is forbidden by society. It is unacceptable. However, my behaviour of going to the toilet is a 'normal', natural behaviour. The circumstances are forcing me to do something in the way I, consciously, don't want to but unconsciously I am being pushed to do it. The natural urge is far more powerful than the knowledge that the action is unacceptable. You can now decide to punish me for my action or you can provide better toilet facilities. If you punish me for my action, the chances are that it will happen again when I find myself in a similar situation.

☐ If an action becomes repetitive, it means that there exists an almost constant energetic stimulus that leads to this action. So, the real question is 'what sensation, what feeling, is creating these recurring thoughts that force me to do the same things over and over again?' I need to change that feeling. I need to change the way I respond to the energetic interaction that triggers me to create that feeling.

☐ If I can't concentrate on what is in front of me, if my attention quickly wonders off, then the question is 'why is my unconscious mind so anxious, so jumpy?' I need to know what I am so afraid of. I need to know what it is that, in the opinion/experience of my unconscious mind, is dangerous to me and can attack me at any moment from any angle.

☐ If I refuse to communicate openly with my outside world, if I am too scared to show my true self, then the question is 'what is so threatening in my surroundings that I have a great need to hide?' I need to know what exactly is so scary about the way my life is developing, the direction I am being pushed into.

☐ The bi-polar wave of emotions is the natural flow of things. It isn't anything 'special'. For some people the amplitude of the wave (how high up and how low down it goes) is much greater than what is considered to be 'the average'. If my natural mood swings are extreme to the point of becoming uncontrollable, then the question is 'what draws me in so deep and locks me into the sensation, the feeling of the moment?' What is happening to me is absolutely normal, only my engagement in the high and low emotions is what makes it different. So, I need to alter the way I respond to these energetic interactions.

Whatever the name of the specific behavioural pattern, it always boils down to an extreme response to a normal pathway. Hence, there is nothing wrong with the behaviour. That, in itself, is perfectly natural. However, how society is functioning and what the leaders and rulers of society want from their subjects, the citizens of the country, of the society they claim to be 'their nation', may make some of this behaviour 'inappropriate'. But when we judge something to be inappropriate, to clarify our opinion, our judgement, we really also need to state in what context it is inappropriate. Why is someone not allowed to be inattentive at times? Why is someone not allowed to be full of energy, full of activity? Why is someone not allowed to be impulsive? Why is someone not allowed to withdraw himself from society, from his surroundings? Why is someone not allowed to quickly change his mood, be euphoric, be depressed?

We fail to acknowledge that behaviour is a learned skill. It consists of two parts. Firstly, there is what the species has learned what their requirements are in order to survive the environment they are confronted with, time and time again. This knowledge is passed on into the makeup of the specific type within a species. In human terms, it determines the various races, each best adapted to their wider environment, both in terrain and climate. Secondly, there is what the individual has learned about what he or she specifically needs for survival in their immediate environment. In other words, how can this specific individual, with that specific set of strengths and weaknesses, survive in the conditions he will encounter in his immediate surroundings, the 'here and now' environment? The taking on board of the information contained in both lessons begins during the pregnancy. First, the human being is formed so it can, physically and mentally, embrace that information, so it is prepared for what is coming its way. This stage is then complemented by taking in, either by copying or by rejecting, reaction patterns of the mother, who is the window onto the future specific environment of the growing individual. After birth, this process continues whereby the baby, the child, further modifies these patterns according to its own experiences. The result is the behaviour of the child. From the point of view of the child, all behaviour is appropriate. From society's point of view, some behaviour will be more 'appropriate', more in line, less clashing, than other behaviour, and society certainly has a preference and wants compliance to what it regards as 'normal'.

As someone who struggles to comply with the rules of engagement set out by society, or as parents to a child who struggles in this way, there is a choice to be made: either one values the requirements of society more than those of the child, or one chooses the child over society. In the first instance, we have behavioural disorders. In the second, we have an individual we need to consider the needs of if we truly want to help the individual.

What is the problem? The problem is an individual who doesn't have enough skills to comply with the life that is forced upon him. There is a mismatch between how the individual has been formed and what life is now expected of him. Hence, there are two different approaches to solve this problem. One is to make him conform, to make him 'normal' again, to help him to be like all the others. The other is to acknowledge that he doesn't fit into his environment, doesn't comply with the norms and values of his surroundings and that his environment needs to allow for this specific individual to be himself. In this case, how the world around this individual is structured and functions needs to be examined as currently there isn't enough living space for that individual. Areas of serious conflicts need to be identified and alterations must be made to allow more room for who this individual is. Behavioural disorder can become behaviour when the environment acknowledges a person for the individual he or she is and makes the necessary compromises to allow the functioning of this individual, in accordance with his makeup, his constitution.

Behavioural disorders are a problem to society. It is a problem, at least the scale of it, which has been created by society. The increasing numbers of 'special needs children', of mental health problems in youngsters, of children with a diagnosis of behavioural disorder, are a warning sign on the road to our future development. We are heading in the wrong direction. A dead end street. No way through.

Chapter 9

Accidents

We all suffer them. However, some people are confronted with more accidents in their lives than others, and some suffer more serious consequences as a result of accidents than others. I have always wondered why. The effects we see that accidents have on our immediate lives are not coherent with the type of accident that has occurred. I have known a man who, coming down from his pigeon loft, missed a step, tumbled down two steps and ended up on the lawn. He was paralysed from the neck down. On the other hand, someone who wrapped his car around a strong tree walked away with a few scratches. I am amazed by those observations and as I now know that, in nature and therefore in life, everything has a reason, I try to understand cause and effect in the case of accidents.

To begin with, it is good to make clear what we are talking about here. An accident is 'an unexpected event, typically sudden in nature and associated with injury, loss, or harm'. It is unexpected. In other words, it isn't planned. One cannot foresee it. It happens spontaneously. As we have encountered in other aspects of life, relating to health issues, something that happens spontaneously is trigged by the interaction of energies. It is, if you like, a natural occurrence, even though we don't see it coming. It is unexpected in the sense that we are not understanding those energetic interactions, are unaware of them, and are therefore surprised by the occurrence itself. It is ignorance that makes us refer to the event as an accident. To nature and the natural forces it is most logical, even unavoidable, and certainly predictable, given the set of circumstances we are in.

It is also interesting to note that sometimes people who either know the victim well, or people who are observing what the victim has been trying to do, comment afterwards on the accident in words like "It was an accident waiting to happen". In other words, these people are not so surprised by what has happened. These people did see it coming. These people seem to have an understanding of the forces that are at work in this specific instance. To them, the event, which is branded an accident, is not unexpected but entirely predictable. So, if some accidents are, to some people, predictable and a logical outcome of what they are watching unfolding, then why don't all accidents have a logical explanation?

Maybe they do, and it is just us who are unable to see the logic, to see the interaction of forces, of energies, that will, inevitably, lead to an accident. And if there is a logic to it then of course the events that are now called accidents will simply become consequences. You were asking for it, now you got it, kind of thing.

Everything in life is about interactions. Nothing creates an effect unless it influences something else. Hence, an accident is the result of an interaction between two or more forces, energies. It is fair to assume that in the case of personal accidents the energies that play a part in the event are on the one hand those of the individual involved and on the other hand the energies in the field that surrounds that individual.

When we inadvertently drop something or we bump our head against the cupboard door, we don't think about an interaction between inner energies and outer energies. Nevertheless, that is what it must be, as all effects are created that way. Why haven't you hit your head against the open cupboard door on all other occasions? Why just now, and only now? What is different in this moment compared to all other similar moments? One could say: "I wasn't paying enough attention". Then the question arises, why not? What was distracting you so much that you didn't notice the open cupboard door? So in terms of interaction of energies, we can identify the following two in this example. On the one hand your conscious mind is busy doing something, fully concentrated on that issue, while your unconscious mind is in conflict with what you are doing at that time, which diverts its attention away from the moment and the circumstances. It may be that you are even aware of the fact that you are resenting 'having' to do this right now. It may be you are doing it but you are really thinking about something totally different. Your mind may be somewhere else! Two diverging energy lines, which results in a 'blank' space in between, a gap in your observation, conscious and unconscious. You never saw the open cupboard door and that is why you bumped into it. You never 'sensed' the open cupboard door. One could say that you were not in the moment.

In general terms, 'the cause' of a personal accident is to be found in the divergence between the conscious and the unconscious mind. One is consciously busy with things that the unconscious mind does not have time for right now or, even worse, knows it is a danger to one's existence. The unconscious mind, experienced mostly as 'intuition', governs life, keeps us safe from avoidable danger and drives us towards the sustenance we require in life. Any serious divergence of energy away from these permanently protected goals is likely, at some point, to create an energetic shortcut, which results in an event that we call 'an accident'. In some occasions we are afterwards able to see the benefit of the accident, which is generally referred to as 'a blessing in disguise'.

Of course, the disguise is only a cover-up for our ignorance.

We will classify this type of accident as an *internal accident*. It is caused by a serious incongruence between energies in the internal fields of the victim, the conscious and the unconscious mind.

Any accident that is the result of our own 'stupidity' is caused by us 'not being in the moment', in one way or another. The result of the accident, the impact on our life, can be immediate and only lasting a short period of time, or it can drastically change our world, and everything in between. Whatever the case may be, it will always be an appropriate effect in terms of what it is achieving. It may simply be a wakeup call where no real harm is done. It may be that certain functions will be affected for a while, in which case one really needs to look at how the harm or injury impacts one's life directly and how one might do things in a different way. Or it may be that irreversible changes have taken place, in which case one is forced to do things in a different way. The interaction, orchestrated by the unconscious mind, results in what the individual truly requires at that moment in life. It is not what he or she wants. The changes the impact of the accident bring stops a specific way of life, one that the individual consciously has been pursuing but one that, as deemed by nature, is a danger to the survival of the individual. It may be a serious invitation to find ways to do certain things differently in life, or an invitation to which changes best to make for the future. In the worse-case scenario, the changes are being made for you. The result of the accident affects you in such a way that life will never be the same anymore.

As all interactions are always appropriate and proportionate, it stands to reason that a life changing impact must be a desperate attempt of your unconscious mind to implement those necessary changes in your life. Invariably, your unconscious mind has had previous interactions with the life you are consciously trying to force and, take it from me, it has been sending you messages. The language used is one of 'not feeling right', or discomfort in a specific part of the body or mind, or smaller, less significant, reoccurring accidents, all aimed at drawing your attention to the fact that where your life is heading right now is not where you need to go. But you haven't been listening. You have become so focussed on what you believe 'to be the right thing' that you no longer can hear the voice of sense, the call of nature. As the danger to your life, to your survival, keeps increasing, so does the power of the energies crashing into one another – messages are becoming 'louder', more obvious - eventually resulting in an explosion with non-reversible effects, but aimed at keeping you alive, even at the loss of certain functions or capabilities.

When we form an integral part of the accident event itself, as in our actions clearly contributing to the event, it is not difficult to see that an inner conflict, creating high tension in mind and body, plays a significant part in what happens. However, there are also accidents that happen to people without them playing an obvious role in the unfolding events. When an aeroplane falls from the sky, people on board are likely to be killed without every single one of them having contributed, in some way, to the technical problem that caused the crash. Walking the way home from work you may well be hit by a car, which is, for no obvious reason, spinning out of control. But there are also examples from the natural world, not just from the human world. Not so long ago, if you were in the wrong place at the wrong time, you might have been washed away by a tsunami in Thailand or in the Philippines. You may be struck by lightning. You may be injured by hail stones or falling rocks. You may be lifted off your feet by a tornado.

If it seems that your internal energies, harmonious enough not to seriously disrupt your existence, do not directly play a part in the type of accident, then you are a simple victim, innocent in all senses of the word. But what exactly are you a victim of? Forces, beyond your own capabilities, 'invade' your space and bowl you over. You do not possess the necessary power to deflect the incoming energy burst. So, the energy that disrupts your harmonics, the energy balance that keeps all elements of the manifestation that is known as 'I' together, is much more powerful than your own personal constructive power. Let's say that the adhesive, that keeps your elements together to form 'I' and to perform as 'I', is not strong enough to withstand the outer energies it is being exposed to. Also, this energy enters your personal energy field from the outside. Hence, once again we have an interaction between your personal energy field and an outside energy field, which can be natural or human world energy in nature. In this instance, it is the force field outside the field of a person, which contains both the conscious and the unconscious mind of that individual. The point is that when such a force presents itself to your personal energy field, it turns out that you do not possess the flexibility and the ability to make the necessary changes, to absorb the effect of the interaction, within the framework of your manifestation. The limits of the way you were constructed become overstretched and the construction, your life, ends or becomes permanently disrupted, in the same way a ceramic dish breaks into pieces if you drop it on the floor.

These occurrences are due to the fact that within the energy field, in which we as individuals form a separate entity, an energy build-up occurs under specific conditions. This can reach levels to which some of the energy entities within that field, some of which manifesting as matter (living or otherwise), have no adequate response. The power, concentrated in this manner as a result of specific conditions, dislodges certain harmonic manifestations within. In other words, it blows them apart or seriously alters their structure and function.

We will classify this type of accident as an *external accident*. Here, the forces that interact with one another are your individual energy field and the outside energy field, which may develop an energy build-up within the human world or within the nature world. The latter fields surround the individual energy field and can therefore be called 'the outside'.

> *To illustrate this. – Whilst talking to a friend we are walking down the stairs together. For no apparent reason I stumble and lose my balance. I fall and inadvertently I push my friend. We both fall down the stairs. Mine is an internal accident and my friend's is an external accident.*

Are we now truly talking of 'an unexpected event, sudden in nature'? The answer is yes, for as long as we don't understand the dynamics of energies, the composition of the relevant fields and the mode of energetic interactions instigating and powering such an energy concentration. In other words, if we were to comprehend the energies in the universe, in the living world, in nature, none of these sudden events would be unexpected. Just as one can see a thunderstorm building in the sky in the specific way the clouds are gathering - once one knows the tell-tale signs - one would not only be able to foresee any major force impacting an individual life, but also one would know the kind of effect it would have on that particular individual, in those specific circumstances. The unexpected event would become predictable, logical and unavoidable.

Just as a good technician can 'sense' that a machine he knows inside out, is not working 'properly', so can insight and knowledge in the energies of nature and of life provide us with a foresight others cannot possess. The main problem of getting our knowledge up to the level of the technician and his machine is that we didn't build this machine, this life. We didn't, consciously, build our bodies or our minds, so understanding them on a deep and intricate level is no mean feat. However, by acknowledging our ignorance about the subject and subscribing to the role of student, whereby we sit still and observe, we undertake a serious step towards a greater understanding. We should not interfere in these processes if we want to find out what happens next. In order to learn about the effects specific interactions have on each other, it is imperative that we do nothing to disrupt the natural way of interacting with each other. Intervention, in any way, shape or form, disrupts this natural process and our essential learning programme. Nature has its way. It doesn't need us to help it along.

The good news is that we do not have to finish the course before we are equipped to act. We do not need to understand all of life before we are capable of making useful decisions about how to support our own life. Adhering to two basic principles, we create the possibility of avoiding many direct confrontations and escalations within our personal energy field.

1. Only information gained from your own experiences is valuable to your own life
2. When something appears to cause harm or conflict stop your action, thought, feeling, that is involved in that specific process at that time

But before we start, let's make one thing clear. There is nothing one can consciously do to avoid an external accident or to minimalise its effect. It is beyond human capability at this point in human development. So I would suggest you stop worrying about it. If it happens, it happens, but living a life in constant fear for an event you cannot alter seems to me a waste of a life. No, let's busy ourselves with the parts of life that we can alter, the suffering that we can alleviate.

Becoming clever about this, becoming intelligent, has nothing to do with thinking. Stop guessing what the message could be, hidden in an event in our life. Things that go wrong or accidents that happen do mean something, but trying to find that answer inside your conscious mind, following logical steps of deduction, is looking for it in the wrong place.

To illustrate this. - One night I was walking home when I came across a man who was clearly looking for something underneath a street light. I asked him what he was doing and he replied: "I lost my keys to the house." So I started looking too. After some time I asked him where he thought he might have lost them. "There by the front door", he answered. In despair, I called out, "Then why are we not looking for them by the front door?" "Oh", he said, 'There is more light here."

Life is a teaching facility and its methodology is personal experience. We learn by doing, by trying things out. Basically it boils down to doing something and observing what effect that creates. Examining the effect, readjusting what we are doing and observing the new effect. Gradually, step by step, we will improve what we are doing. And what if 'what we are doing' is how we believe living a life in harmony, at peace with ourselves, should look like? Well, if your life is truly in harmony, you will be free from disease and accidents.

Any event in our life, any accident, will have an effect on the action we were engaged in. Don't ask the question 'why' this happened. Observe what the effect is on what you were doing. What does it do to you? And how does that effect impact what you were doing? Now realise that 'something' is telling you to stop doing that or stop doing it in that way. Acknowledge that signal and give it credit.

The next step is to remember what you have observed and not to repeat that 'mistake'. Think about doing it differently and execute that thought. Don't worry about doing 'the right thing'. In learning, there is no such thing, just as a stupid question doesn't exist. All you need to figure out, through trial and error, through experience, is how to handle life and the changing balance of life as it presents itself to you. What does life show you as the priorities in your life? Not what society or your friends tell you. No, what are you experiencing as the priorities in life. Observing what life shows you is a good way of approaching your life in general terms? What does life show you as the best way for you to handle conflicts? Well,

- change your habits, your thoughts, your beliefs, your convictions, and your feelings to match those messages as best you can. - don't be disheartened by so called failures. Failure is how we learn. That is when we pay extra attention.
- keep repeating the method: experience – observe the effect – change – experience – observe the effect – change - ...

So simply by observing the circumstances and the effect of those circumstances, as seen by us, we can learn how things work. 'Why' is a different matter altogether. The answer to the 'why' question we will become aware of once we have had plenty of well observed experiences. In our analysis and restorative actions we will first go through a number of 'false' changes, changes that don't lead to a permanent balance in life. Only by going through these stages and following the path of learning through experience can we become sure about what it actually is that is 'right' for oneself. Life, and living it in the right way, is a marathon, not a sprint. It is all about the long term. Hence, one will have to stay on the case!

Accept accidents as a proper way of communicating with the unconscious.
Avoid accidents by following the instructions from your unconscious GPS system.

Chapter 10

Trauma

According to the American Psychological Association, trauma is 'an emotional response to a terrible event', such as an accident, rape, or a natural disaster. People may experience trauma as a response to any event they find physically or emotionally threatening or harmful. This means that the experience is what it is, but it is how the individual *responds* to the experience that is the trauma. This makes trauma a very individual thing. There is no way in which the personal impact of an event can be measured and extrapolated to the entire population. It is impossible to equate the gravity of an event to the trauma a person experiences as a result of the event. Even so, a major trauma, in physical medicine, refers to 'a severe physical injury caused by an external source', without any reference to the response of the individual. In medicine, they have chosen to call the sustained injury the trauma, rather than the response to the sustained injury. This is a specific choice, that lifts the reality of trauma out of the psychological and emotional realm and into the physical, out of the realm of personal responsibility and into the realm of victimisation.

Not everyone who experiences a stressful event will develop a trauma. The event can cause a range of emotions both immediately after the event and in the long term. People may feel overwhelmed, helpless, or shocked and may have difficulty processing their experiences. This kind of response can also lead to physical symptoms. Symptoms that persist and do not become less severe can indicate that the trauma has developed and has a destabilising effect on mental health, called post-traumatic stress disorder (PTSD).

Traumas can occur in three different ways:

- Acute trauma: This results from a single stressful or dangerous event.
- Chronic trauma: This results from repeated and prolonged exposure to highly stressful events. Examples include cases of child abuse, bullying, or domestic violence.
- Complex trauma: This results from exposure to multiple traumatic events.

The way a trauma manifests in the daily life of a person varies greatly as it is an individual response to an event. Each individual can potentially express his or her ongoing distress in a very personal way. This may be through emotional disturbances, psychological aberrations, behavioural oddities, and even physical symptoms such as headaches, digestive symptoms, fatigue, tachycardia and palpitations, sweating. Sometimes, a person will also experience a constant state of alertness. This may make it difficult for them to sleep.

According to the World Health Organisation research from 2017, about 70% of people worldwide may experience a traumatic event at some point in life. Many charities and other help organisations produce lists of 'traumatic events', blaming the events for the effects certain individuals experience in response to these events. All of this is of course simple bullshit!

There does not exist such a thing as traumatic events, and at the same time any event can be a traumatic event. The reason for this is that the event itself is only an event and the impact it has on the individual is what is causing the trauma. It is how the person experiences the event that causes the trauma. In the same way that a certain comment may be experienced by some as a good joke and by others as an insult. The comment itself is not responsible for how an individual chooses to respond to it.

Blaming the comment, blaming the event, even though it may have been unavoidable as is the case for a natural disaster, serves a purpose. Blaming is to identify a person or situation outside of ourselves in order to avoid holding ourselves accountable for the negative situation or occurrence that has taken place. By making the event responsible for the trauma reaction of the individual, we absolve the individual from any guilt or blame for what happens to him and for the consequences that follow. We remove all guilt and responsibility for something that went wrong from the 'suffering' individual and place it outside of that individual. But what happens when we avoid responsibility? Not taking personal responsibility can have a negative impact on our mental health. It can lead to feelings of guilt, shame, and anxiety, which can be damaging to our emotional wellbeing. We may start to feel helpless or trapped in our situation, leading to a sense of hopelessness and depression. Not taking personal responsibility leads to exactly the same expressions we have called a trauma.

A trauma is the direct result of a person not taking responsibility for his own life. It is not about taking responsibility for what has occurred, as the event itself may happen totally outside of someone's personal power to stop it from happening or to alter its course. No, we are talking about taking responsibility for your own reaction to the event. The way you feel about it, the impact it has – in other words, what it does to you – is your responsibility. Why? Because you generate all your own emotions, feelings and thoughts. If you are afraid, it is because your system has generated the feeling of fear. That feeling has not been implanted into your life from an outside source. It may be a reaction to something outside of you, but in that case that is your reaction, which means that nobody or nothing else is responsible but you. Acknowledging this responsibility is the first step towards ensuring a trauma never happens to you or when it does, when an event takes you by surprise, that you are able to wash it out of your system quickly.

Putting the blame outside of the individual and rendering the individual the victim of a traumatic event, rather than the subject of an event, opens the field of all kinds of supporting therapies. Several treatments can help people who are experiencing trauma or PTSD cope with their symptoms and improve their quality of life. Doctors will select a treatment that best suits a person's situation. Medications may help a person to manage symptoms such as anxiety, depression, and sleep disturbances. Doctors may suggest selective serotonin reuptake inhibitors (SSRIs) such as sertraline (Zoloft) or paroxetine (Paxil).

Therapy is a preferred treatment for trauma. People can work with a therapist who has experience handling trauma. Beneficial types of therapy may include:

• Cognitive processing therapy (CPT) - a specific type of cognitive behavioural therapy that involves 12 to 16 one-hour sessions.

• Eye movement desensitisation and reprocessing (EMDR) - During EMDR, people briefly relive specific traumatic experiences while a therapist uses bilateral stimulation, which may involve eye movements, tapping, or other stimuli.

• Written expression therapy - During this type of exposure therapy, a person writes about the traumatic event and pays close attention to the thoughts and emotions they had at the time of the event.

• Accelerated resolution therapy (ART) - an emerging therapy that has shown effectiveness in significantly reducing PTSD symptoms in veterans.

• Somatic therapies - Some therapists may use somatic (body-based) techniques to help the mind and the body process trauma. One example is somatic experiencing, in which a therapist helps someone relive traumatic memories in a safe space.

Practising self-care can help people cope with the emotional, psychological, and physical symptoms of trauma. Examples of self-care for trauma include:

• Exercise - A 2019 review suggests that aerobic exercise may be an effective therapy for people with PTSD.

- Mindfulness - A 2021 study suggests that mindfulness strategies may help reduce the negative effects of cumulative trauma in U.S. veterans.
- Social connection - The U.S. Department of Veterans Affairs suggests that social support is one of the most effective methods to protect against PTSD.
- Sleep - Traumatic experiences may contribute to sleep difficulties. Most adults need 7 to 9 hours of sleep per night, so a person may benefit from speaking with a doctor about how to improve their sleep.

Recommendations by professionals in the know. Recommendations that make constant use of words such as 'may' and 'suggests'. No recommendations filled with certainty, with knowledge. Nothing that has even a reference to what causes the trauma.

Lots of help on offer. Lots of suggestions about things that might help. No information on why a person becomes traumatised by an event or a series of events. The medical profession is creating a great number of specialists, each with their own 'special' approach to the problem, attempting to make people feel better. None is concerned about helping to lift the individual out of the trauma state he finds himself in. They are quite happy to proclaim: "Symptoms of trauma after a stressful event are common. Seeking help from a healthcare professional can help people manage their symptoms and emotions. In some cases, trauma may develop into PTSD. However, doctors can prescribe medications and therapy to help a person manage the condition."

All about helping to manage the condition. But, once we recognise what a trauma is, where it originates from, we can quite simply work out a strategy to remove trauma from our lives.

We follow a few logical steps in our approach.

- Recognise it is you who creates your response and therefore your trauma
- If you don't like the effects of your response, you can decide to change your response
- No longer empower your feelings, emotions, about the event
- No longer empower your thoughts, assumptions and analyses about the event
- Allow yourself to approach the event as another occurrence in your life, like so many other events.

It is just an experience, and its value is no more or less than that of any other event.
- Empower a neutral position towards the eventually
- Accept the fact that the event taught you something about life

Will you get over your trauma? Well, that depends on you. You may not want to hear it but it is your responsibility to manage your own life. You can make different choices in life. You can decide not to feel hurt, not to be angry, not to feel disheartened or helpless. You can decide to feel grateful for the lesson, to feel empowered by the experience, to feel the responsibility for your own life.

When you no longer see yourself as a victim of life, you can participate in life without fear. It is not possible to enjoy life when you fill it with fear. Shit happens, but do you have to care about the shit happening? Who cares? If you don't, if you are not afraid of shit happening, you won't live life anticipating disaster after disaster. If you accept that shit happens, you won't become traumatised by life.

Childhood trauma

But what about children and their traumas? How can those be explained and understood?

'Child trauma' refers to a scary, dangerous, violent, or life threatening event that happens to a child (0-18 years of age). Once again, who decides and on what basis, that a certain event is scary, is dangerous, is violent or is life threatening? And once again, it is said that the event itself is the trauma.

It is the interpretation of the event that determines the status of the event as scary or dangerous or violent or life threatening, not the event itself.

In this respect, they define a 'traumatic event' as a scary, dangerous, or violent event. An event can be traumatic when we face or witness an immediate threat to ourselves or to a loved one.

So, if I see a loved one nearly falling of his bike, that is a traumatic event in my life!

When this happens, it can cause emotions such as fear, loss, or distress. Sometimes people experience these types of strong negative emotions in reaction to the experience or because the person may not have the ability to protect or stop the event from happening. Reactions to a traumatic event can also have lasting effects on the individual's daily functioning including possible changes in a child's mental, physical, social, emotional, and/or spiritual health.

*And now all of the sudden, it **is** the reaction to the traumatic event that can cause all the harm!*

Children who suffer from child traumatic stress are those who have been exposed to one or more traumas over the course of their lives and develop reactions that persist and affect their daily lives after the events have ended. Traumatic reactions can include a variety of responses, such as intense and ongoing emotional upset, depressive symptoms or anxiety, behavioural changes, difficulties with self-regulation, problems relating to others or forming attachments, regression or loss of previously acquired skills, attention and academic difficulties, nightmares, difficulty sleeping and eating, and physical symptoms, such as aches and pains. Older children may use drugs or alcohol, behave in risky ways, or engage in unhealthy sexual activity.

Before we get lost in the emotional forest of 'poor child', we might do well to remind ourselves as to what children truly are, in energetic terms, and how life during that time is structured. They come into this life with a rucksack full of knowledge, gathered throughout history by their ancestors, by their tribe and by their family. Not only do they have a good idea about what life is like on the outside, but they also come prepared for that specific life. They have reaction patterns at their disposal that will help them to survive in those circumstances. Armed with all of that, they face the reality of that outside life every day, from the day they are born. And all the time, unexpected things may be happening. As they experience things, they use the automatic reaction patterns they have, so they can deal with these events. Every unexpected event can be listed as scary, dangerous, violent or life threatening, because the child doesn't know how these will progress and what these events really mean. Not knowing is scary. But as they are trying out different reaction patterns in response to these events, they learn more and more about the dynamics of each event and about the usefulness of their reactive responses. Through the experience of new, unexpected, scary, dangerous events, the child will get to know more about the reality of life itself.

Another aspect of how the child reacts and learns to pick the most appropriate response to an event is by observing and copying the adults around it. Children take their cue from their trusted environment. So, when a child, years after a specific event, is still troubled by either the memory of the event or by anything that remotely looks or feels like it, it can be that way only if the environment of the child shows the child that this is an appropriate way to deal with the event, by for instance, holding on to the memory. To a child, losing a loved one can only become a trauma when its environment is unable to let the passing of that person go. In nature, we might see a very short period of time where the animal looks a bit confused, disorientated, but soon it gets on with life, focuses on food and survival. And that is what children do, using their natural reaction patterns, if left to their own devices.

'When children have been in situations where they feared for their lives, believed that they would be injured, witnessed violence, or tragically lost a loved one, they may show signs of child traumatic stress.' Indeed, they may show signs of stress. – Apparently 'traumatic stress' is stress as a result of witnessing a traumatic event! – Indeed, when a child that has just gone through what to them is a scary situation, they may well show signs of stress. But once they are in a safe environment again, the stress subsides. That is how nature works. It is not the child that keeps holding on to the fear it experienced in that scary situation. Their environment has now become so fearful of it happening again that measures are being taken to prevent such a situation from ever occurring again. Now the atmosphere around the child is filled with fear and those are the frequencies the cells of that child are encountering all the time. This continual fear signal sets off alarm bells within the child and the entire organism now acts as if there is a constant threat in the environment. It isn't the child who turns one event into a lifelong trauma. It is that part of society that 'supports' the child that does that for the child. The more 'protective' measures are being taken, the more the child 'has to be careful', the more fear energy that will fill its life.

But we are so lucky the medical profession has treatments available. Some children may not recover from trauma on their own, even with family support. In these cases, a mental health professional trained in evidence-based trauma treatment can help children and families heal. Over the last two decades, the demand for and availability of evidence-based treatments (EBTs) for children under the age of six who have experienced trauma has dramatically increased. Three of the most well-supported and widely disseminated EBTs for early childhood trauma are Trauma-Focused Cognitive Behavioural Therapy, Parent-Child Interaction Therapy, and Child-Parent Psychotherapy.

Even though the problem is an inappropriate automatic response to a given event or situation, their preferred therapy is 'cognitive' based, which involves a process of thinking and reasoning. They propose to solve an inappropriate response, coming from the unconscious mind, by using the logical capabilities of the conscious mind. Apart from the fact that the conscious mind is incapable of understanding the unconscious mind, apart from the fact that life is an energetic happening and not an intellectual one, how effective will this approach be in making the conscious mind of a child, aged six or under, see reason in how inappropriate its reaction is? As far as parent-child interaction and child-parent psychotherapy is concerned, both take as their starting point that the problem is the child, and it is the child that needs fixing. In fact, the system of the child only acts in a spontaneous natural way and is therefore always 'correct' in its response, taking all energetic aspects into consideration. If you want the child to respond differently then you need to 'feed' it different energies. You will need to change the energetic environment of the child, and that entails changing habits and routines, changing thoughts and convictions, changing judgements, changing goals and means to achieve those goals. There is your effective therapy! Treat the environment of the child and the child will respond appropriately.

The reality of life involves times and situations that are scary, dangerous, violent and life threatening. That is the reality of life. That is normal. Coming across those at an early age only allows the child to learn valuable lessons early on in life. And yes, that is hard, but at least it is honest. The consequence of being protected from those sorts of situations and not coming in contact with them allows the child to grow up with the idea that life is easy, is nice, is comfortable, is safe. But whether you as a parent or a responsible adult like it or not, that image of life is a lie, and when you protect your child from events that in our modern day are called traumatic events, you are doing it a disservice. You deny your child the right to decent copying mechanisms, to effective reaction patterns. If you don't teach your child these, it is you who will be responsible for the trauma in the young adult life of your child.

Childhood trauma can potentially contribute to various mental illnesses in adults, including post-traumatic stress disorder (PTSD), anxiety disorders, depression, and borderline personality disorder (BPD). The severity and type of mental illness may vary depending on the nature, duration, and frequency of the trauma, as well as the individual's genetic predisposition and coping mechanisms. It is important to recognise that not everyone exposed to childhood trauma will develop a mental illness, but the medical profession says it increases the risk. This so called 'risk increase' is the direct result of observing two events - in this case, childhood scary, dangerous, violent and life threatening events and adult health problems – on the basis that you believe there must be a causal link between the two. However, there is no mysterious link. Life is simple. If you adopt one reaction pattern, which becomes an automatic response to a specific impulse, which may be an event, a situation or a simulation (either real or imagined), and you don't change it then it remains the same. In other words, if, as a child, you have learned to respond in a specific way then you will continue to respond in that way as an adult, until you become aware of the fact that you can actually change your response. And even more importantly, you are the only one that can change it!

A childhood trauma is caused by the behaviour and the emotions of the adults around the child.

Adults affected by childhood trauma can learn how life is structured, how it functions and how their own conscious mind can be used to change their reaction patterns in life.

Chapter 11

The Stages of Life

This seven layered nature can also be found in the life of every human being. It is all structured in the same way, following the same rules of engagement. So now let us see if we can make the connection.
Remember this:

1	water/skin tissue	lymphatic system
4	blood tissue	circulatory system
6	muscle tissue	digestive/respiratory system
2	fat tissue	mobility system
5	bone tissue	sensory system
7	nervous tissue	nervous system
3	reproductive tissue	glandular system

Seven different tissues and seven different systems, each an expression of a specific energy phase, which we have identified with the figures 1 to 7. An energy phase is like a musical note. It has a 'meaning'. It conveys a message. It holds information. Each of these energy phases holds information of a specific nature, which can be expressed in physical matter that is distinctly different for each phase. The information contained within the various energy levels has been identified.

1	creating form
4	creating balance
6	creating consciousness
2	creating movement
5	creating communication
7	creating knowledge
3	creating personal power

We can now see how the systems and the tissues within the systems are a manifestation of this energetic information. It gives 'meaning' to the physical expressions. It shows what kind of energy is manifesting through what kind of physical matter.

1	form	water/skin tissue	lymphatic system
4	balance	blood tissue	circulatory system
6	consciousness	muscle tissue	digestive/respiratory system
2	movement	fat tissue	mobility system

5 communication	bone tissue	sensory system
7 knowledge	nervous tissue	nervous system
3 power	reproductive tissue	glandular system

Because of the work described in the book *'Why Me? – Science and Spirituality as inevitable bed partners (ISBN-13:9789082785425)* by Dr Patrick Quanten & Erik Bualda', we know the relative contributions of each of these energy phases to the different layers of the living matter. From this, we have been able, amongst other things, to calculate the lifespan of a human life, bearing in mind that there are lots of impacts on the way, which can either lengthen or shorten specific phases of life due to less or more pressure exerted by that specific energy. But it gives us an idea of what the spectrum of human years looks like and it allows us to verify our calculations by the various phases human life passes through, comparing that with the changeovers in energy phases. The total lifespan of an individual is 98 years, including the gestation period. The gestation period is calculated from the moment of conception, unlike the medical gestation calculations, which start on the first day of the last menstruation, in effect two weeks before the conception takes place, with a margin of error of 2 to 4 days. So, the real gestation period in humans is 38 weeks.

The figure of 98 years certainly falls within the lifespan of an individual human being. Looking at the energy behind the creation and the manifestation of a particular life we need to concede that the actual length of life is dependent upon a lot of factors interfering with that life. The evolution of an energy field may speed up or slow down, compared with an 'average' and depending on the amount of pressure there is on that individual life it will either run faster or slower through the various energetic deployments of each layer. This will shorten or lengthen life, or, in more general terms, the designated time period, calculated within the framework of a model. Reality is always different from any model or any theory we may come up with. Each of the following phases of life may vary in time for each individual. However, the phases life runs through will always remain the same and will have a length of time in the region of the calculated framework.

As we are dealing with energies and the manifestation of energies, these figures, and the corresponding timeline, must be seen as a guideline rather than absolute points in time. Every manifestation at every level may shift slightly in the timing of its appearance and for how long it will hold out before the next energy level takes over. This can affect the actual length of time the individual is affected by each of the seven layers, including the foetal development. However, the model may allow us to learn a bit more about the evolution of a human life in function of the influences of various energetic phases.

How the life of the individual evolves, which energies last a long time and which are burned quickly, will result in a longer or a shorter life. What is interesting, however, is how the changeovers from one energy level to the next relate to the age of the individual.

1	ends at about the age of 3	infant - toddler
4	ends at about the age of 8.5	child
6	ends at about the age of 17.5	teenager
2	ends at about the age of 32.5	young adult
5	ends at about the age of 56	adult
7	ends at about the age of 95	elderly person
3	ends at about the age of 97	death

Each of these stages in life are well recognised because the individual behaves differently, has a different focus in life. And it turns out that each of these stages are representative of a specific energetic influence.

1 formation of that life; giving it a certain shape (partly as foetus, partly as baby)
4 finding a balance between personal shape and the shape of the environment
6 becoming conscious of personal shape and the shape of the environment
2 finding one's own way; being 'on the move'
5 communicating with the environment; personal experiences to gather knowledge
7 knowledge about personal and surrounding development; being sure about what you know
3 focusing on personal needs

Let's take a closer look at the development of a human being as he goes through the various stages of life. We can identify the following stages in relation to the various energy levels at every stage of life:

1 - embryo	1	creates the basic human shape
	3	creates the basic personality
- foetus	4	balances the new individual with its environment (the energies of mother)
- baby	6	creates an awareness of the self and its surroundings (mother)
Birth		
- 6 months	2	develops mobility
- next year	5	develops communication skills with its environment
- next 18 months	7	develops knowledge of how 'to be' (= to survive) within
its environment		

(energy phase 1 is composed of the seven energies, manifesting in the order 1-3-4-6-2-5-7)

4 - finds a balance between having its needs met without antagonising its environment

It is based on this learned knowledge and the learned way how to deal with it, that further life will develop. This represents the foundations of an individual human life. It is on this solid ground that the individual will build his life. This stage ends at the age of about 3.

6 - awareness of the structure of self and the structure of the environment

This awareness creates the first conscious 'clashes' between the individual and the world that surrounds him. How he responds and how he deals with the reaction from his environment to his behaviour will shape the kind of choices he will make, the kind of steps he will take towards an independent life.

2 - mobility; both in the physical reality and mental/psychology reality a move away from the homestead, from the 'family ways'

5 - communication, learning how 'to explain' his inner world to his outer world and learning how 'to read' and understand the outer world

7 - knowledge; a personal way to view the outer world and the inner world, based on his own experiences and on his own personal reaction patterns, which he has used all his life

3 - knowing that all that really matters is 'me'

The basic formation of a new human life, the foundations on which that life is going to proceed, is completed by the age of three. From then on the child, teenager and young adult will be using the learned skills and knowledge about how 'their' world operates in order to navigate the potential dangers of that world. The growing individual will be testing out the learned reaction patterns he has encrypted within his unconscious mind. Some of these reaction patterns he has been 'given', has copied, and he will use them in order to survive, when he moves away from the school he has been attending. The young child, and certainly from the teenage years onwards, will mainly absorb information from its surroundings in order to expand and fine tune its learned reaction patterns. When it encounters big anomalies between the reaction pattern it has learned and the observed unexpected result, the child may either slightly adjust the reaction pattern or it may hide, being afraid of encountering similar situations again. That is the start in life the child is getting. To a certain extend protected, but at the same time limited in its scope. On the one hand, the safety and protection of prison walls, but on the other the restricted freedom of the same prison walls.

The individual now has a personal way in which he 'sees his world' and knows how to deal with it. This is this specific person's reality and how he must respond to it. Gradually, through various experiences and by evaluating the effects his reaction patterns produce, he will be able to expand his knowledge about life in general. In principle, he does have a chance of readjusting and improving his life in relation to the natural world, from which he came and to which he fully belongs. In principle, because the reality is that it is very difficult, scary and unsettling, to contemplate the idea that your lifelong reaction pattern is inadequate or even simply wrong. We start life with the tools we are handed by our predecessors, in the form of genetics and learned (copied) knowledge. As we use those tools, we can observe how effective they are and where they are not serving us well in an ever changing world. This allows us, usually later in life when we feel more secure in ourselves, to make adjustments that will improve our own life and that will contribute towards the knowledge of humanity as a whole. We are passing the knowledge of our experiences on to the next generation by changing the learned reaction patterns and showing others something different. Our experiences, our gathered 'knowledge', create slight changes in the balance of the human energy field – it adds something to it - which remains in existence after the death of an individual specimen. One consequence of this is that the human being born in a different era will have a built-in knowledge of what went before. This hands him the tools to deal with what comes next, and establishes the evolution, in this case, of mankind.

All of this makes every phase in life really important, and that includes dying. It is a very important experience for a human to have, as it is the point where all the jumbled up experiences are neatly ordered and filed to be passed back into the human energy field. The time leading up to the natural death of a human being is a crucial time for awareness. Becoming aware of what is really important in life as opposed to what younger people, all wrapped up in a very small portion of life, want to believe life is, and is a small window for humanity to have a sneak view on reality. They say: "With age comes wisdom!" Wouldn't it then make sense to listen a bit more to old folk?

But they are all demented! They talk rubbish because they do not understand the modern world. Yes, and as far as the modern society is concerned, they start talking rubbish at an ever earlier age. Senior doctors are being dismissed because they question the validity of certain medical procedures.

Senior scientists are being laughed at because they no longer seemed to understand the new science. Senior factory workers are being sidetracked because they feel the company is getting too big for their boots. Senior politicians are being replaced by baby-faced, slick talking, mechanically sounding, holier than the pope, little robots. In general, there is no further use for senior citizens in our modern society. It is so obvious that society is even offering them a way out, a way out of their misery, a misery caused, but not recognised, by society itself. There is a purpose to old age, but it is no longer being valued by society. The only purpose for a human being society recognises right now is an economic use. What is your contribution to the production and the trading market? If you are not contributing enough to the *common purpose*, you are a burden to society. Hence, they make euthanasia available and promote it as a blessing for old folk, whose only existence is one of suffering. Society puts on a caring face and proposes to puts these suffering animals out of their misery.

As they are trying to lighten their own burden of not only having to care for these useless human beings, but also potentially, having to come face to face with, to them, such disturbing knowledge about life, they have turned their attention to tackling the problem at the source itself. As the first years of life are so formative it becomes extremely difficult for a human being to change its learned patterns later on in life, it makes a lot of sense to gain control over babies as soon as possible. Putting the control of very small children in the hands of official institutions, regulated in all aspects, allows the authority to inscribe behaviour patterns unto these new lives. In the UK, multiple authorities and organisations play a role in baby development, with a focus on different aspects of care and support. The Department for Education oversees the Early Years Foundation Stage (EYFS), which sets standards for learning, development, and care from birth to 5 years old. Ofsted regulates and inspects early years providers, ensuring they meet these standards. Additionally, the Department of Health and Social Care and the NHS play significant roles in providing health services and support for babies and their families. Organisations like the Unicef UK Baby Friendly Initiative and the NSPCC also contribute through specific programmes and resources. Be aware that in terms of human evolution, all of these are very very new. These are, what is called, recent developments for the wellbeing of the child and its parents. We are so lucky that such authorities finally came into existence, given the great parental stupidity young children have been exposed to for a few million years. Humanity nearly didn't make it in the absence of such authoritarian organisations. Or so it seems, through the eyes of all these experts who are telling parents what their children need. The effect of this massive assault on babies, infants and toddlers is to impose learned reaction patterns, belief systems and thinking patterns that align with the ideas and aims of the authority, thereby undermining the individual and direct influence of parents, family and local environment. The natural learning pathways of very young children are being filled with a chosen set of information and behavioural patterns that allows for the creation of equal human beings, as well as for the disappearance of individuality, of diversity, of connection to local reality, of inclusiveness, of tolerance, of real life knowledge.

The demise of humanity begins with the creation of a gap between the individual and his own experience of his environment, life as he feels it. When the individual is no longer allowed to make up his own mind about how he encounters life and what that means to him, humanity is losing its most important source of information, its driving force of evolution. By detaching human beings from the reality of their lives, one cuts them off from their senses. One is able to manipulate the conscious mind of individuals, but the unconscious, which is an essential part of life itself, can only be tricked for a short period of time. Once one strays too far from the natural path, there will be a pull-back reaction from nature that will not take no for an answer. Life will survive. Evolution will continue. And humanity, guided by its arrogant stupidity, will suffer. But it will also survive, because there will be elements within the human race that will make their way back to the reality track of life.

Life will continue to pass through those seven stages, no matter what any authority tries to do to it. Life will continue to be confronted with reality, no matter how hard any authority tries to control what that confrontation looks like. Life will continue to create individuals who are immune to whatever poison the environment may hold for them. Life will continue with those who face the reality of nature, rather than the reality of virtual truth and of predicted futures. Life will continue on its natural path, rather than following a computer model or algorhythm predictions. Eventually, life will expose the power crazy arrogance of child-like authorities. Worshipping images rather than life itself will come to an end. Death awaits us all, including the ones who are trying to conquer it.

Be happy with the thought of you dying one fine day. Be calm and enjoy the unique view you will have on life itself. It is a sunset you really don't want to miss.

Chapter 12

Moving Forward

So there you have it, life as an energetic process. This was the reason I invited Patrick back to Cornwall for one last fling, to get to the absolute foundation of the human experience. By understanding the simple forces that creation uses to manifest its potential and the nature of the human mind, we can now start to see life, and its challenges, in a new way and start to understand 'cause and effect' in a new way, and especially the part we play personally in the 'cause' but especially in the 'effect'. The *cause* is mostly out of our control although with changes of awareness and behaviour we can affect this to an extent. The *effect* is where we can make a real difference in that we can, if we like, choose our effect to the incoming information, the cause.

For me personally, I see two ways this information can be used and by two types of people. In our book '*A Conscious Humanity – Morality, Freedom and Natural Law*' we explained in simple terms the so-called 'matrix' that humanity is locked into. We compared the geographical map of the world, with its laws of nature that are fixed and the direction nature is going into, to the political map with its man-made illusionary laws that vary from country to country. We also talked about the fact that all political systems are directed to one destination, the total control of the human population.

Seeing through that illusion is the first step to take back control of our lives. There now seems to be two types of people in the 'awake' community that need this information to move forward in their lives. The first type is the individual, family or community, who can see the grip the illusion has, but for various reasons are not able to escape it. They have certain health, financial or physical reasons why their personal situation means they are dependant and reliant on the system and the best they can do is to create a bubble of freedom within the control system. This bubble can give them enough freedom to express their inner needs and give them enough freedom to remain in balance. The second type is the individual, family or community, who can also see the illusion but are determined and have the personal or group power to do something about it. They don't just want to survive but want to push for freedom, at least a lot more freedom, and this requires being self-reliant and not being dependant on the system. These people want enough freedom to pursue their own personal life balance and evolution, free from unreasonable restraints.

So my question for Patrick is, based on this information regarding the forces of nature and the human mind:
What advice do you have for each type of individuals going forward and what information do they need to look at and implement to try and maintain their own personal balance?
What realistic results should each person expect if they start to turn inward and trust their unconscious mind?"

Before anything else, I think it is important to understand that there is no good or bad way to respond to the pressures of life. Human beings have always lived life being pressurised by humanity, or more specifically by a group that considers themselves to be 'the elite'. Over millennia and in all parts of the human world, the composition of this group has varied, but there is always a dominant group of people at every corner and every turn of the history of humanity. So much so that we now believe that without an authority, people cannot live together. What does that say about those individuals who strive for less dependency on the system and for more self-reliance?

Self-reliance is defined as 'the quality of not needing help or support from other people'. Well I can tell you now that that isn't going to happen! There are very few people who truly have the capacity to live completely by themselves, without any help from anyone else. If we look at it slightly differently, we could define self-reliance as 'confident in your own abilities and able to do things for yourself'. Now that sounds more plausible. And then the idea is to become more independent of the system, less reliant on the system. So, you want to look after yourself, without the system dictating you what to do?

You take care of your own food, your water, your energy requirements, your shelter. That will do it! No, it won't. You also need to provide your clothing, shoes, tools, protection against forces of nature, but also against coercion, manipulation and violence from the system. Maybe you are going to need some help after all. Many hands make light work. But wait a minute, you are not done yet! You also need to take care of your own health. You also need to determine what is right and wrong for you, without relying on a justice system or a preset morality system. You also are a registered person within the system you are trying to escape from. You have a name that belongs to the system. You, for instance, will have to pay taxes and social insurance contributions, even when you pretend not to belong to the system. You will need a bank account, and for that you will need a residency address. It appears that the system has tentacles in every aspect of your life. Anything you don't have or can't provide for yourself, you will have to get from the system. You will need money for that. How are you going to get money? If you want to sell something, you will need a licence from the system. It turns out that being independent from the system is not going to be as easy as that.

No wonder a lot of people, who have woken up to the fact that the system isn't what it appears to be, are not bothered about leaving the system and are simply trying to find a way to survive within the system. Most of us have responsibilities towards other people too. Some other individuals do find the need and the strength to stand on the barricades and to try and fight their way out of the system. However, all their efforts will confront them with the next layer of attachment to the system. There will be resistance all the way. There will be opposition all the way, and not just by the system, but more importantly by the people who believe the system is providing them with a life and who don't want to see their lives being jeopardised by the actions of other 'irresponsible' human beings. It will be an uphill struggle, but bit by bit progress will be made, even if it takes three generations to truly get to the top of the hill, to the gates of freedom.

You may now have the impression that there is no escape possible for the majority of us, victims of the 'elite' system. There is, however, another aspect to this system. I have already mentioned that, even though the system has remained in place, the composition of the ruling elite has changed many times. This is the result of the fact that, no matter how strong and secure the setup appears, it always collapses. Inside it goes rotten. What first is a good idea and works well, becomes exploited and corrupt. Every empire or emporium, be it political or industrial, has collapsed, and so will this one. Thus far, humanity has only managed to replace the old one by a new one, following the takeover by another elite group. Could it possibly be different this time?

For that, we need people to be awake, but even more so, to be ready. It doesn't matter that much how individuals are living right now, whether they are in their own created bubble believing they will survive, or whether they are truly on the barricades for freedom of the individual. What matters is their mental preparedness to let go of what the system is offering. To each individual reaching that point of no return, it will be a different journey, but what matters is that they are awake enough to recognise that the basic concept of the system will not change by changing the masters. We need to ditch the system if we want more personal freedom, if we want more personal independence. And then it doesn't matter anymore if you are making this transition all by yourself or as a small group of people, altruistic willing to help each other. Freedom from the system truly means setting up a life whereby you no longer take notice of what the system does or wants you to do. It means taking full responsibility for everything that happens in life, and that includes diseases, old age and death.

Readiness to take full responsibility, when the system cracks. When the fence around the system no longer is strong enough to hold the diversity of human lives together within one coral, no longer providing that sense of security against the supposed dangers from an unknown outside world, the fence breaks in places. It is those gaps that are opening up for people to escape through, while the elite is too busy trying to manage an increasingly more nervous and anxious population. For the ruling faction, the only tactic left in that situation is to divert attention from the broken fence. So, if you are looking to escape, if you are looking for a 'different' world, then find the cracks and use them to your advantage, but remember that what works for you may not be good enough for someone else. Just be patient. Others will climb over the broken fence in their own good time. Others may use different cracks to find their way out. It's on the other side you need to meet up in order to create a new reality without authority, without a ruling system.

A question for me regarding my own personal passion in helping children. Many parents now all over the world, especially in the so-called developed and civilised world, are struggling to cope with their children's 'behaviour disorders'. For those who have read this information and want to bring it on board to try and understand and create a better balance for their children, what is the best and most simple advice you can give? In many countries there are limitations on parental power, with examples like having a choice to vaccinate or not, or to home-school or not. It seems that we cannot win all battles against the system but is there anything specific you would say as to when parents should be the oak tree and when they need to be the palm tree?

That is the crucial point. Especially when we are talking about parenting, which is taking responsibility for the lives of your children. Stand too long in the firing line and you will get shot, in which case you are no longer able to take responsibility for your children.
So it will be a journey of carefully putting one foot in front of the other. I would suggest not to attack the system, but instead to try and use the limitations of the system. Stand on your right and that of your children when the system is simply 'assuming' the right to implement things, when in fact they have not got that right. Get to know the law, rather than the rules, with regards to education. Don't be fixed on schooling, but open your mind to what the law says about education. That is a different thing all together. Place this alongside what official organisations, international as well as national, proclaim on children's right and on parental rights. Find inconsistencies and use those to protect your child from interference by the authority. For example, when the school is putting forward a

vaccination programme you don't agree with, you write a letter in which you explicitly state you don't want your child to be vaccinated, and if it does happen, you will sue the school for assault.

The state, backed by supra-international organisations, will override every rule and every human right in the name of a worldwide 'potential' disaster. Hence, when they go all out for the children, no manner of protest will stop them. However, the bigger they make the pressure dome to include as many people from as many walks of life as possible, they also increase the combined resistance against their policy. They have observed that in the aftermath of Covid, when they let everything settle down to evaluate the real changes in attitude amongst the population. In those scenarios, you are never alone and people should really seek out other parents with a similar mindset, who find themselves caught in a similar fashion. Look for a solution that suits you all at that moment in time, but stick to one specific point of grievance. Do not be tempted, or don't allow yourself to be forced, into a fight with a more general theme. In the example above, that could be not allow it to become a discussion whether or not you are for or against vaccinations. Keep the focus on your parental right to decide what you feel is right for your child, not the school, the school nurse or the government medical advisor. If, in this case, you get threatened by not being allowed to send your child to school, you accept that. When the child is effectively dismissed from school, you make an official complained to the government because your child is being denied an education, while the government underwrites the Children Rights Act, which says that every child has a right to an education. One step at the time. Wait for something to become real before you react. Only fight the one point you are making, nothing else.

Maybe to some of you it is also worth pointing out that one of the reasons why individuals, adults and children, are an easy target for the government is the fact that we are registered within the system. They know everything about all of us. If we stop engaging within the system so much, we can reduce their immediate power over us. Don't use a smartphone. Don't use a credit or debit card. Don't shop in supermarkets. Have a limited use of the internet. In other words, don't google stuff all the time, but use a library instead or ask a person you trust for his opinion instead of an 'influencer'.

And the ultimate bit of awareness is the fact that in all countries the laws and rules hit the local population the hardest. If you are a foreign national, with a foreign bank account and an income from abroad, there is a lot more room to play with. Have you ever thought how the richest, the most influential, people in the world contribute so little to any society anywhere and why they, seemingly, are free from prosecution, relatively speaking? It is because they don't stay in the country they are born and raised in. They don't register their life in one country.

They 'spread themselves' thinly across the globe, whereby various governments and authorities get bits of them but never all of it. That way they still hold on to a great deal of control over their own life.

I know it isn't the thing to do for all of us but knowing that this is how it works may help you, either to make more appropriate decisions for yourself and your family or to be at peace with the fact that others are managing to organise more freedom and independence in their life than you are.

Whatever you do, you need to be at peace with your life, with your decisions in life, and with the fact that you don't have the power to find 'the right solution' to every problem you encounter in your life.

Understanding what energy, in nature terms, truly is and how it operates, leads to the question, 'what do we do with this knowledge?'

We know we are part of an unfolding of universal energies. It has a beginning, a direction and an end destination. We as individuals play a very small, but none the less, important role in this journey of unfolding and developing energies. There is an old saying *'ask and it shall be given',* which in a way translates into the famous equation $E=MC^2$. The physical part of life, M, is equal to the energetic part, E, and it is the energetic part that creates the physical part (It is the biggest!). Like you have said, if we want to change the physical, the energy has to change first. There is also another saying *'ask and it shall be given, but be careful what you ask for as you just might get it'*, which refers to what the conscious mind is asking – how the conscious mind understands reality – which gets translated into a different form by the unconscious mind, reflecting the reality of life. You may get what you asked for, but not in the form you had imagined it to come to you.

It seems to me, the unconscious mind knows what it **needs** and looks out in the environment for energies to help fulfil that need. The conscious mind knows what it **wants** and does the same within its limited scope. However, 'wants' and 'needs' of a person may not be the same. This again shows the importance of going within and trusting in intuition coming from the unconscious mind, connecting to real 'needs' rather than to desirable 'wants'.

With the world politically going towards a system of total control, we also can highlight another famous saying, *'you feed what you fight'*. So the energy of fighting flows towards the object of the battle, thereby energising whatever it is you are obstructing or opposing. It is also clear that the people behind the system are actually provoking various fights to hand themselves excuses to create their idea of *order out of the chaos*, a chaos they themselves have created. So would it make more sense to try and energetically disengage from the system rather than to fight it? To focus on the world we want to create rather than the world we want to avoid, so that we are feeding the new world via our focus, using our energy directly for creation rather than for destruction. As Gandhi stated *"be the change you want to see in the world"*. Gandhi also spoke of 'village republics' in that every community, large or small, was totally in charge of its own organisation. Being careful to acknowledge this is the alleged 'gift' of big government in the form of devolution. Their version of this is local responsibilities, directed by people trained in the philosophy of central control, referring to every problem as 'much larger than their own local community'. This system of devolution ensures an even greater central control, whilst maintaining the illusion that *it is local communities governing themselves*. Truly independent local government means that a specific local community does not have to follow what another community decides. This allows for the natural diversity to manifest and to grow roots of history in every single community that are different from anywhere else.

So is all that we can really do in life is just focus on what we want to create and detach from what we want to avoid?

*No. There isn't much point in focussing on what you want if you don't understand what nature, the universe, you, actually need. If what you want, wish for, to happen in your life contravenes where your life truly is going and what lesson you really **need** to learn right now, then all you will achieve with 'your want' is inner conflict. First, you need to learn what life in its natural form really is and how that functions before you can effectively manifest what it is that you **need**, and not your wild, unnatural desires.*

But as far as you and the big outer world is concerned, you may notice that the construction and the priorities of that world don't match the nature of life. Enforcing such an unnatural life will create conflict with human life, within the life of individuals. Hence, they become unbalanced, both mentally and physically. They become ill, malfunctioning, and die at an early age. Or the individual senses this and starts resisting this enforcement, thereby moving the conflict into the outside world, rather than allowing it to upset his own inner world. Now the individual is 'fighting' the system, or parts of it. In doing so, he/she is empowering the system to take more control, because the system has educated people to believe that there can only be peace and harmony after one has won the war. Hence, a justified, hard hitting mobilisation of policing and enforcing agencies is welcomed by the population. One against all, is not a fight the individual is going to win, especially not when all his efforts only result in more support for enforcement and stricter control.

These individuals could do better for themselves and for humanity. They could, where possible and each in their own local situation, powered by their own personal strength, not oppose the authority but focus their attention on two very different, but extremely important, other life issues. One is that, where possible, one decides no longer to commit acts that hand power to the authority. For instance, if you no longer make use of the medical facilities provided by the authority, you are no longer being haunted by their protocols. If you no longer use a smart phone, you are no longer subjected to any mind control that is conducted via those devices. Secondly, rather than putting your energy into fighting for 'justice' or for truth and honesty within government, you could simply begin, where possible, to create a different life for yourself and your family. You could make up your own rules of engagement amongst yourselves. You could create your own 'morality', your own kind of religion, simple rules of 'do's' and don't's'.

Engaging your energy in creating your own life, rather than being dependent upon an authority for all necessities in life and for all decision making in life, is going to empower you rather than the controlling authority.

*Directing living your life towards a life based on the Laws of Nature, studying through observation and questioning the way Nature functions, will increase your personal power, power over your personal life. Nobody **needs** power over someone else's life. And people who voluntarily decide they want to join their lives together always take the requirements of the other person into account. If you don't, you are not living your lives together. You are living 'with' each other without being together. And together, you can then decide what the priorities of that life will be and how life will be conducted. Together. Not one person commanding someone else.*

*We can use the effects our unconscious mind produces as indicators as to where our individual life is going, where Nature **wants** to take it.*

Links

If you find all of this difficult to follow or difficult to put into practise, don't despair. Everything we come across for the first time appears difficult to us. Difficult simply means 'unusual', but unusual on a personal basis. What is easy, routine, to some people appears impossible to others. So all we really need to do is to make ourselves familiar with the 'new' thing, in order for it to become less difficult.

As far as this theoretical material is concerned, it helps if you read up on it and you keep being faced with the same concepts over and over again. You can also introduce the same information in different formats, in different frameworks. To help you with this, you can visit the websites www.pqliar.net and www.activehealthcare.co.uk. These will provide you with a variety of material that helps you to look at life in a different way. A comprehensive and detailed study of the Laws of Nature – how Nature works and what that means for humanity – can be found on the website www.quantics.org. Here you can also express your commitment to studying life and truth, and to learning what you need to do in order to create a life of balance, rooted in universal truth. By becoming a member you join a group of people who, each individual in his/her own life and own circumstances, is trying to create a better world for themselves, and by extension, for humanity. A world without domination. A world where the only authority is Nature and the reality it expresses to us. A human world in line with the natural world.

Patrick's 4 part seminar 'Your Health in Your Hands' and the 13 part series of follow-on conversations can be found for free at the YouTube channel of Rob Ryder https://www.youtube.com/@robryder3505/videos

The same content plus two more interviews with Patrick regarding medical science can be found at the Rumble channel https://rumble.com/user/robryder
Other publications by Patrick Quanten and Rob Ryder:

Little Miracle Baby: The Perfect Life of Kennedy Jack
– Patrick Quanten

Why me? - Science and Spirituality as inevitable bed partners
– Patrick Quanten and Erik Bualda

Your Health in Your Hands: How to be healthy in spite of "medical science" –
Patrick Quanten and Alicia Ninou

A Practical Guide to the Restoration of Health
– Patrick Quanten and Evelyn Scott

Medical Despotism: The health, economic and political programme that can kill you
– Rob Ryder and Patrick Quanten

A Conscious Humanity: Morality, Freedom & Natural Law –
Rob Ryder and Patrick Quanten

DEBT SLAVERY: The Economics of a Banking Mafia - EDITION 2 –
Rob Ryder

Awareness and well-being guided journal: And the truth shall set you free
– Rob Ryder

www.ingramcontent.com/pod-product-compliance
Lightning Source LLC
Chambersburg PA
CBHW061233070526
44584CB00030B/4108